Greenlicious Cookbook

SIMPLY VEGAN - SIMPLY DELICIOUS - SIMPLY NOVEL

Dominica Collis & Gary Collis

Title: Greenlicious Cookbook, Simply Vegan - Simply Delicious - Simply Novel

First published in 2022

ISBN (paperback): 9798411178494

For Dear Ann

This book
is dedicated to YOU.

We hope that our recipes will make you
fall in love with cooking
and take you on a mouthwatering adventure.

Dominica & Gary xxx

Contents

WELCOME

Welcome   5
About this book   6

Health benefits of a plant based diet   8
From our kitchen to Yours   14
Equipment   17
Cupboard & Fridge/Freezer essentials   19
Herbs & Spices   26
Fresh Produce   29
Our recommended suppliers   30

RECIPES

Breakfasts   33
Lunchs & Dinners   53
- Eastern European
- Indian
- Mediterranean
- Mexican
- Oriental
- Traditional British

Sauces & Dips   189
Desserts   205
Drinks   223

FINAL WORDS

Welcome

CREATING MAGIC IN THE KITCHEN

We would like to take you on a little journey and introduce you to our way of making life in the kitchen that little bit more interesting whilst keeping it simple but producing the most delightfully delicious dishes.

In this book we will introduce you to some simply scrumptious plant-based meals that we have created. Both wholesome homely dishes and tantalising restaurant grade feasts to treat your family and friends too. Everyday is a new day for us and we are always batting new ideas off of each other and creating new meals daily of which we are going to share some of them with you.

When we very first started cooking together it did not take us long to realise that we both just flowed working in the kitchen. Our ideas just complimented each other's and we soon found, it was a place for us to grow together and deepen our relationship and we certainly had lots of fun in the process and continue to do so. There is something special about creating magic in the kitchen with the one you love.

And now we want to share that passion with YOU and make you fall in love with all the delights that vegetables & fruits have to offer.

D&G X

About this book

WHY WE DECIDED TO WRITE IT

We decided to put this book together because we love spending time in our kitchen. It is a space in our home where we combine our energy and love for cooking relatively quick, healthy and scrumptious meals. Over the years we have built quite a collection of cookery books that have been both educational & inspirational, however we both realised that our style of cooking is very eclectic and we often combine different cuisines to create our tantalising meals.

We both really dislike food going to waste and this is where we started looking at using the surplus from the meals we cook to create something completely different the following day.

Our aim in writing this book is hopefully to inspire YOU with the meals we create, and for you to become creative in your own kitchen and to not be afraid of trying new things. In this book we will be creating some meals where we cheat a little and will be using things like pizza bases, various breads and some select cheeses, all of which are vegan with very simple ingredients that just aid the speedup of the prep to plate time (we will indicate on the recipes where we cheat a little, which is totally fine but of course if you wish to make these things from scratch you can but you will need to add additional time & ingredients to do so).

"Dominica has been vegan for almost 11 years and I made the decision to join her over 2 years ago. I literally went vegan overnight and have my beautiful wife to thank for making the transition so easy. I can honestly say it has been the best choice I have made and I now live a much healthier and happy lifestyle. At first I thought cooking plant based meals was going to be dull and boring, how wrong was I, once Dominica started sharing her extensive knowledge on plant based cooking, well that's really where the journey began for me and oh how my taste buds were in for a surprise."

Gary

"I absolutely love how we both flow together in the kitchen. Of course, initially Gary was completely new to vegan cooking, but he has always been curious, not afraid of experimenting, and loved cooking, so very quickly we were creating new scrumptious meals based on our ideas".

Dominica

Another message we hope to get across in our book is that cooking meals at home does not have to be complicated nor expensive, whether it be a comforting homely dish or stepping it up a gear and creating a restaurant grade dish to impress your guests, use this as a opportunity to learn and don't be afraid to make mistakes as this is how we grow in the kitchen and become more confident, you can always correct the mistake on the next attempt or until you perfect the dish you are cooking. We will also be giving you some insight into our kitchen, the herbs & spices we have to hand, our cupboard essentials & the fresh produce we like to have stocked in our fridge.

We are confident that if you are prepared to cook outside of the box and take a few risks, you will discover just how simple it is to make both restaurant grade and soul satisfying meals in the comfort of your own home in no time at all.

We are excited about seeing your creations, so please tag us on our Instagram @greenlicious.cooking

Health Benefits of a plant-based diet

Definition: A whole food plant-based diet (WFPB) is one consisting of fruits, vegetables, whole grains, legumes, nuts, seeds, with few or no animal products.

'Well-planned plant-based diets can support healthy living at every age and life stage. Include a wide variety of healthy whole foods to ensure your diet is balanced and sustainable.'

The British Dietetic Association (BDA)

Poor diet is now the number one cause of death and disability in the UK and many other countries all over the world (1 in 5 deaths globally every year, around 11 million deaths in total), resulting in a rising burden of chronic disease, obesity, cardiovascular disease, dementia, liver disease, type 2 diabetes and cancer. Unhealthy diets are typically too high in saturated fat, sugar and salt and certain animal-derived foods, like red and processed meats; and insufficient in healthy plant-based foods.

Benefits of a Whole Food Plant Based Diet

A WFPB diet has been shown to reduce the risk of these diseases, improving health and longevity.

Obesity and hypertension - compared to omnivores, those eating a WFPB are more likely to have a normal BMI and lower blood pressure (BP). A WFPB diet low in salt can be as effective as medication in lowering BP.

Cardiovascular disease - 30% decrease in cardiovascular mortality (WFPB can reverse atherosclerosis).

Cancer - 15% decrease in cancer incidence and may improve survival after a cancer diagnosis. Mechanisms include lowering IGF1, avoidance of haem iron and decreasing the production of carcinogens.

Type 2 diabetes - 60% decreased risk compared to omnivores. In those with diabetes, a WFPB diet improves glycaemic control better than standard approaches and can even reverse the disease and improve end organ damage.

Dementia - Shares the same risk factors as cardiovascular disease, which are improved or avoided with a WFPB diet. Healthy lifestyles could prevent a third of cases.

Non-alcoholic fatty liver disease (NAFLD) - 21% decreased risk for those on a plant-based diet. NAFLD is strongly associated with obesity, insulin resistance, diabetes and cardiovascular disease.

Improved longevity - those eating predominantly plants, live longer and healthier. WFPB diet increases telomere length, which protects DNA.

Emotional and mental wellbeing - WFPB promotes a healthy gut microbiome. These friendly bacteria produce unique chemicals, short-chain fatty acids, that act in the brain and provide a sense of well-being.

Improves fitness - phytochemicals and antioxidants reduce inflammation and produce faster recovery times and pre-training fitness.

Nutrition

One thing that often concerns those interested in a plant-based diet, is that they worry that they will be missing out on essential food groups by adopting this lifestyle. And if you are not open to trying out new foods, textures and tastes, then this could hinder your chances of getting all the necessary vitamins and minerals. But nature does provide us with everything our body needs.

Proteins

Plant-based proteins are found in beans, peas, chickpeas, lentils, nuts as well as soy products such as tofu, tempeh, edamame, soybeans or dehydrated soy chunks or mince.

Plant-based proteins are healthier than animal-based proteins because they are low in fat, and high in fibre, protein, vitamins and minerals. They keep your body tissues in good health, build, maintain and repair your muscles, bones, skin and blood, as well as regulate hormones and enzymes, and fight infections. Our clever bodies are able to make eleven of the amino acids that are necessary for these functions, but the other nine can be found in the food we eat.

Most adults need around 0.75g of protein per kilo of body weight per day. On average, this is 45g for women and 55g for men. As a guide, a protein portion should fit into the palm of your hand, and unfortunately, many people eat way more than that, which is detrimental to their health.

To start with, for main meals, swap out meat for beans, pulses, lentils, or chickpeas. Ensure you eat a portion of raw unsalted mixed nuts per day (30g). Plant-based meat alternatives can be a good option for those wanting to transition to a more plant-based diet. However, they are processed food and contain high amounts of salt, sugar, saturated fat and additives so should be restricted to occasional use.

Fibre

Fibre, found exclusively in plant foods, is essential for supporting healthy and regular bowel movements, helps keep us satiated, regulates our cholesterol and hormones, and supports the health of our gut microbiome. With many medications (antidepressants, antiepileptics, antipsychotics, opiates, diuretics, calcium and iron supplements) and diseases (hypothyroidism, irritable bowel syndrome) causing constipation, often laxatives are recommended, but they are harmful in the long term use. Fibre prevents constipation and has no side effects.

Aim to eat at least 30g of fibre daily by basing meals and snacks on whole fruits, vegetables, beans, pulses and whole grains. Swap refined grains like white bread or pasta for whole grains: brown, red or wild rice, whole wheat bread, pasta and couscous, teff, amaranth, quinoa, millet, pearl barley, einkorn, spelt or oat groats, bulgur and buckwheat.

Calcium

It can be easily obtained from dark green leafy vegetables, tahini, fortified non-dairy milk and yoghurts, legumes, calcium-set tofu and seeds. It helps to build strong, healthy bones, muscles, and nerves and ensures that the blood clots properly. There is no negative effect on bone health if dairy is avoided.

Omega-3 Fatty Acids

Obtaining enough omega-3 fatty acids from the diet, in the form of alpha-linolenic acid, is important for plant-based eaters. Plant sources include walnuts, flax seeds, hemp seeds and chia seeds. Algae derived DHA/EPA supplement may be a good option, especially in pregnancy, breastfeeding, for children and older adults. This avoids the pollutants in fish, such as mercury, dioxins, polychlorinated biphenyls (PCBs).

Vitamin D

Vitamin D is mainly made by the action of the sun on the skin and food sources are generally poor. Foods fortified with vitamin D can be a useful source of vitamin D and you can find it in many non-dairy yoghurts and milk nowadays. A supplement is recommended for all during the winter months. Choose a plant-based source of vitamin D3, as it's an active form of vitamin D and helps to raise the levels more efficiently than vitamin D2. It is a fat-soluble vitamin, meaning that it does not dissolve in water and is absorbed best in your bloodstream when paired with high-fat foods. For this reason, it's recommended to take vitamin D supplements with a meal to enhance absorption.

Vitamin B12

Conversely to the popular belief that vitamin B12 is made by animals, it is actually made by microorganisms in the soil. Animal products, however, are the usual source of vitamin B12, simply because they eat livestock feed fortified with B12, as well as grass with soil. It is responsible for the upkeep of nerve and blood cells, and the production of DNA.

It is crucial for everyone on a plant-based diet to ensure they have a reliable source of Vitamin B12. There's a great choice of fortified foods that you should consume 3 times a day, i.e. nutritional yeast, a popular and very tasty ingredient in our recipes, plant-based milk and yoghurt, Marmite or other yeast extracts. You can also supplement (we recommend an oral spray) at 10mcg daily or at least 2000mcg weekly.

Iron

It has been suggested that the avoidance of haem iron, found in animal-derived foods, may have a beneficial role in cancer, diabetes and cardiovascular disease. Good sources of non-haem iron include blackstrap molasses (our no #1 choice), legumes, seeds, dark leafy greens, dried fruit, oats, quinoa and some fortified foods, which should be consumed ideally with sources of Vitamin C to enhance absorption, i.e. salads or quinoa seasoned with lemon or lime juice.

Selenium

It is an essential trace mineral that supports many bodily processes. It can help improve cognition, immune system function, regulate and balance thyroid function. It can be easily found in plant-based sources including brazil nuts, cashews, oats, sunflower seeds, brown rice and beans. Just two brazil nuts will provide your daily requirement.

Zinc

Zinc is a micronutrient that plays a key role in the growth and immune health. Good plant sources of zinc are beans, lentils, tofu, tempeh, miso, whole grains, wholemeal bread, nuts and seeds. Phytates in grains and beans can reduce zinc absorption, however, soaking, fermenting and sprouting can increase absorption.

Iodine

A daily supplement containing up to 150 micrograms in the form of potassium iodide or potassium iodate may be advisable - especially for preconception, pregnancy and breastfeeding because iodine plays a critical role in early brain development. Some plant-based milk is fortified with iodine. You can also find it in seaweed and our choice is dulse, wakame, kombu, or nori. Always choose organic seaweed, which has been tested and quality checked for heavy metal toxicity.

References

1. GBD 2017 Diet Collab.Lancet. 2019 S0140-6736(19)30041-8

2. Bodai B.I. et al. Perm J 2018 10.7812/TPP/17-025

3. Tonstad S, et al.Diabetes Care. 2009;32(5):791-6

4. Yokoyama Y, et al. JAMA Intern Med. 2014;174(4):577-87

5. Satija, A. et al.. J Am Coll Cardiol. 2017; 10.1016/j.jacc.2017.05.047

6. Kim H. et al Am Heart Assoc. 2019 10.1161/JAHA.119.012865

7. wcrf.org/dietandcancer/exposures/wholegrains-veg-fruit

8. Ornish D, et al. J Urol. 2005;174(3):1065-9

9. Barnard, N et al. Am J Clin Nutr. 2009; 89(5): 1588S–1596S

10. Li Y, et al. Circulation. 2018;138:345-355

11. Melina V, et al. J Acad Nutr Diet. 2016;116(12):1970-80

12. Seidelmann SB, et all. Lancet Pub Health 2018 S2468-2667(18)30135-X

13. Wilson Tang, WH. N Engl J Med 2013;368:1575-84

14. Rosenbaum M. et al Obesity 2019 10.1002/oby.22468

15. Manzel, A et al. Curr Allergy Asthma Rep. 2014 Jan;14(1):404

16. Losasso, C. et al. Int Journ Antimicro Agents 2018 1 2018.07.023

17. Doré J et al. Curr Opin Biotechnol. 2015 Apr;32:195-199

18. gov.uk 2016 Eatwell Guide: colour PDF

19. Ornish D, et al. Lancet Oncology 2013 S1470-2045(13)70366-8

20. Barnard N. et al Nutrients 2019 10.3390/nu11010130

21. Livingston, G et al. Lancet 2017; 390:2673-734

22. Mazidi, M. and Kengne, A. Clin Nutr, 2018 10.1016/j.clnu.2018.08.010

23. Agarwal, U et al. Am J Health Promot 2015 29[4]:245–254

24. Dinu, M. et al. C Rev Food Sci Nutr. 2017 0408398.2016.1138447

From Our Kitchen To Yours

We believe that a kitchen is the most important room in your living space, regardless of shape or size it needs to be made a place where both magic & fun can occur at the same time.

Whether your kitchen is small and cramped or large and expansive, a clever layout will make all the difference in helping you to get the most out of the space. A kitchen needs to flow, allowing for ease of access to both the tools you are using and the food you are about to prepare.

Here are a few tips to help you really master your kitchen and cooking skills.

Ensure that your kitchen, cupboards and fridge are organised to ensure the right flow

We absolutely love labels and all our jars, containers, and bottles are labelled. We tend to organise our cupboard shelves into categories like 'grains & pasta', 'beans & pulses', 'flour & baking', 'sauces & condiments', 'nuts & seeds', 'syrups & sweeteners', and of course 'tea & coffee'. Having a separate spice rack in a close proximity of the hob is also very helpful, as you can easily reach out for what you need anytime. If you buy herbs and spices in bulk, as we do, ensure that your little jars are also labelled for ease.

Always keep fruit and vegetables to hand

Aim for a rainbow in your fridge. Having it nicely stocked will always make cooking from scratch easier. Don't worry, if you bought too much fruit. Portion them, freeze and use in smoothies or homemade ice cream. Too many vegetables? Cook a chunky vegetable soup or stew and freeze, or simply pop fresh veggies into a container or a freezer bag and freeze.

Majority our recipes presented in this book can be easily frozen and served at the time you need it.

Always aim for an improvement

Treat each recipe as an opportunity to learn something new. Observe how the flavours change as you add herbs and spices. Try to feel the food with your senses, the textures, the aroma, the taste, the look. There are so many wonderful videos, Instagram accounts, cookbooks, where you can learn new cooking skills, whether it's improving your knife skills, making meringue with aquafaba (chickpea water) or going more advanced into making a fresh tomato consommé.

Knowing how to cook gives you freedom and independence and is incredibly rewarding. And remember, because it applies to everything in life *"We're never perfect; we are all work in progress."*

Equipment

The equipment we use to help prepare our food is our personal preference and there is a good selection of manufacturers out there making them. We suggest researching the items and taking time to read the reviews if you are looking to equip your kitchen and find the ones that best suit your needs/budget.

Essential items

- A good, selection of sharp knives (and sharpener)

- A sturdy chopping board that looks great and inspires you to cook. Believe us! There's nothing worse than a wobbly chopping board!

- High-powered blender (we absolutely love Vitamix, but there are alternatives like NutriBullet, Blendtec or Ninja)

- Food processor (we use Magimix, but Ninja is also particularly good and is ideal for small kitchens as their Ninja Kitchen System combines 3-in-1: a vegetable chopper, food processor and blender)

- Spiraliser will allow you to create a completely new experience on your plate with courgette spaghetti ('courgetti') or carrot pappardelle. The possibilities are endless!

- Pestle & mortar - we cannot imagine our life without one, as there's nothing more aromatic than freshly crushed seeds added to your meals!

- A selection of mixing spoons, spatulas, tongs - silicon or wooden ideally to prevent scratching the non-stick pans and pots

- Rolling pin - the heavier the better

- A selection of non-stick saucepans, pots and wok

- Measuring tools, like kitchen scales, measuring jugs and spoons

- Ovenproof dishes in various sizes

- Springform cake tin and tart/quiche tin

- Pizza trays

- A selection of different size mixing/salad bowls

- Steamer or bamboo steaming basket useful for your oriental dishes, as well as warming up wraps, pancakes or steaming vegetables

Good-to-have items

- Mandoline slicer perfect for shredding, slicing and creating julienne strips of fruit and vegetables

- Glass containers for storing surplus food in the fridge; use BPA free plastic containers or bags for the freezer

- Juicer - we highly recommend slow or masticating juicers (we use Green Star Tribest Elite Juicer), but there's a great selection available at various price ranges; there's nothing better for breakfast than a glass of freshly pressed nourishing juice!

- A tofu press is helpful to use with the medium firm or extra firm tofu to remove excess water and create an even better texture for your meals. Don't let it stop you from making tofu dishes if you haven't got one yet, simply place the tofu block between two plates and squeeze with your hands.

Cupboard and Fridge/Freezer Essentials

Having the right, versatile and tasty ingredients at hand is the most crucial step in going on that greenlicious cooking adventure and preparing your scrumptious plant-based meals. You may already have some basics in your kitchen. The list below will help you grow your vegan larder over time. These are the ingredients that we use personally and having them really helps to create delicious and balanced dishes effortlessly.

CUPBOARD

Beans

One of the great things about beans is that they cross cuisines; they are a staple in many countries and cultures. They also come in a ton of varieties - there are over 400 types of beans. And that's just what we know is edible. You have a couple of options:

Ready-to-eat tinned beans and we always recommend buying organic with minimum ingredients and look out for the firming agent - Calcium Chloride, as it may irritate the gut lining and Sodium Metabisulphite, which is a preservative, that triggers respiratory issues and asthma-like allergy

Dried beans - our first choice; they come much cheaper, if you buy a kilo or two, there's no added copious amount of salt or nasty preservatives, the only downside is that you will have to soak them for a minimum of 12 hours before cooking, so it requires some planning

Lentils

Puy, red, brown or green. They are an excellent replacement for mince in Bolognese, shepherd's pie or lasagne. Lentils are really versatile, filling and can be used in countless different dishes depending on the spices you use. You can buy them pre-cooked or dry. We buy them dry in bulk, i.e. 2-3kg, which comes in much cheaper and goes a long way. All lentils, but red split ones, have to be soaked before cooking though, so you'd need to accommodate it in your meal planning. Once cooked they can be stored in the airtight container in the fridge for up to 4-5 days.

Peas

We like to have frozen garden peas or petit pois at hand, because it's a great addition to many meals, including stews, soups, salads, sauces.

Soya chunks and mince

Soya is a great source of 'complete' plant protein, very rich in isoflavones, a type of antioxidant, that helps to help minimise the damage known as oxidative stress, done by molecules called free radicals. It's this oxidative stress which is involved in both ageing and the onset of chronic disease. It has a perfect 'meaty' texture, too, that takes on the flavour of herbs and spices that you use. Always buy soya from organic sources, because it's mass-produced (it's used in the feed for farm animals) and heavily sprayed with pesticides, herbicides, fungicides etc. or genetically modified.

Nuts

There are so many... walnuts, pecans, Brazil nuts, cashews, macadamia, almonds, hazelnuts, pistachios, pine nuts.... All of which have one thing in common: they are extremely nutritious and rich in the essential fatty acids: Omega 3 and 6 that are necessary for many bodily functions, but particularly a healthy nervous, hormonal and cardiovascular system.

They all taste differently and are used for different things, i.e. we use cashews to make cheesecakes and cream, almonds are beautiful in homemade milk, walnuts, pecans or pistachios simply sprinkled over a salad, ice cream or added to smoothies.

Seeds

Sunflower, pumpkin, sesame, chia, flax... Seeds are underestimated, but they're full of vitamins, minerals and healthy fats. They can be added to porridge, stews, sprinkled over salads, stir-frys, used in smoothies as a milk replacement, the list is endless.

Nut and seeds butter

You probably already have peanut butter, but did you know you can get others? Cashew, almond and hazelnut are all so incredibly delicious.
And, the best news is that some companies are now offering seeded butter and our absolute favourite is pumpkin seed butter!

Dates

Dates are a source of bone-friendly minerals including phosphorus, potassium, calcium and magnesium, as well as iron and fibre. There are many different types, we usually buy Medjool, Deglet Noor or Mazafati. They are a lovely snack or sprinkled over the porridge or yoghurt but due to their moisture content, they act as a perfect binder in raw vegan cake bases, energy balls, flapjacks, etc. We call them "nature's caramel".

Dried fruits

It's great to have a selection of dried fruits in the cupboard, even if it's only a small bag. They are incredibly healthy. One piece of dried fruit contains about the same amount of nutrients as the fresh fruit but is condensed in a much smaller package. By weight, dried fruit contains up to 3.5 times the fibre, vitamins and minerals of fresh fruit. We especially like to have dried apricots, figs and cranberries, that we often sprinkle over porridge or use in bread or raw vegan desserts. Preferably buy organic, or at least avoid sulfur dioxide, a commonly used preservative in dried fruits.

Miso

This fermented soybean paste is a Japanese staple ingredient, offering a deep umami flavour. It's a wonderful ingredient to have at hand if you want to enhance the flavour of soups, stews, sauces, salad dressings. A simple soup of diluted miso is hard to beat as feel-good comfort food.

Vegetable stock powder

We love having it in our cupboard because having a bouillon on hand simplifies making a soup, stew, or even a broth.

Nutritional yeast

Fortified nutritional yeast is a vegan-friendly source of complete protein, B vitamins and trace minerals required for optimal health. It has a unique savoury flavour that resembles cheese, making it a great alternative for adding flavour without salt, sugar or fat. It's available in health food shops and many supermarkets nowadays.

Grains

It goes without saying... grains are a crucial staple of a plant-based diet and there's a massive choice from the obvious rice (white, brown, arborio, basmati, jasmine, Thai, red or wild), quinoa (a 'complete' protein source) or its cheaper but equally nutritious alternative - teff to millet, pearl barley, einkorn, farro, or buckwheat (our favourite that you can get in a raw or roasted version). And that's not the end of this list, as oats, polenta, couscous and pasta also come into that category. Not all pasta is vegan, so avoid any with eggs or coloured with squid ink.

Tamari and soy sauce

They are relatively interchangeable, however, soy sauce would be overpowering in some cooking methods, but because tamari contains twice the amount of soybeans instead of wheat grains, it results in a richer, deep soy flavour while soy sauce tends to be thinner, lighter, and contain more salt.

Tahini

This savoury condiment is a staple across the globe, originating in Middle Eastern and Mediterranean cuisine. It's also found in Asian and Greek dishes. It contains more protein than milk and most nuts. It's a rich source of B vitamins, iron, magnesium and vitamin E. Apart from using it in hummus, or salad dressing, where it adds not only flavour but also creates creamy smooth texture, it can also be used in marinades, cakes, dips, sauces and smoothies.

Coconut milk and cream

Tinned coconut milk is a perfect addition to soups or sauces and we like to have a couple in our cupboard. Coconut milk is different to coconut cream, which is much thicker and creamier, and perfect to use in desserts, like ice cream or cheesecakes that require that smooth and rich texture.

Natural sweeteners

There are so many! We often use maple syrup in our desserts and cooking due to its rich mineral content. Certain recipes require a different texture, so we also have a bag of coconut sugar and agave syrup, which is light in colour and is most suitable for certain desserts.

Lucuma powder is a great alternative to use in low sugar desserts. Our favourite is Sugavida, a palmyra blossom extract, which is the only plant that naturally contains vitamin B12.

Blackstrap molasses

A great binding ingredient for homemade flapjacks, granola, power bars. You can also drizzle it over your porridge or yoghurt. It's a fantastic iron supplement.

Marmite / Yeast extract

Marmite and yeast extracts are incredibly healthy and rich in vitamins B1, B2, B3, folic acid, and B12. Enjoy it spread over your toast, or use it as a rich flavour enhancer in sauces, soups and gravies.

Quality oil

Depending on the requirements you may want to have a selection of oils in your cupboard. Stock up on cold-pressed flaxseed oil (a wonderful source of Omega 3), hemp seed oil (both Omega 3 and 6 fatty acids) and extra virgin olive oil, as they are amazing in salads.

Walnut oil and toasted sesame oil are a must-have for your Asian dishes. Organic rapeseed oil or extra virgin olive oil both have a high smoke point, which makes them suitable for frying.

Seaweed

Helps you get a fishy, salty flavour. We use many different seaweed types as they are very nutrient-dense and our favourites are wakame, dulse, kombu and nori.

FRIDGE & FREEZER

Tofu

A soya-based 'meat' alternative. Choose firmer varieties for cooking or silken for sauces and desserts. Plain tofu will nicely soak up flavours if marinated for an hour or two. You can also find many already flavoured and marinated varieties in the supermarkets. Our recommendation is to always buy organic tofu. The Cauldron brand is great.

Tempeh

Similar to tofu, but it's made from fermented soybeans. It's firmer with a stronger flavour. It's very healthy and we like marinating it overnight to allow it to fully absorb the herbs and spices.

Plant-based milk

You can easily make your own at home for a fraction of the cost, and we often make almond, cashew, hazelnut or oat milk. Most health food shops and supermarkets now offer a great selection of plant-based dairy alternatives. Our favourite is Minor Figures Barista oat milk, Provamel and Rebel's Kitchen.

Dairy-free cheese

There are many brands now available in every supermarket. Tastes vary, so if you don't like the first one you try, keep trying others! Our absolute favourite is M&S Plant Kitchen range, especially Feta cubes. Coconut oil is the main ingredient in most vegan cheese offered in supermarkets, so eat them sparingly.

There are also many smaller artisan cheesemakers that you can find on websites like The Vegan Kind, Alternative Stores or meet personally at various vegan events across the country. Many use nuts or seeds as the main ingredient, so it's a much healthier alternative.

Yoghurt

This is a must-have in our fridge. They are made from soy, coconut or almond and are available as natural or in a selection of fruity flavours. We use yoghurts in our salad dressings, dips, curry sauces & for breakfast with our granola and fruits.

Vegan butter

Look for the range of dairy-free butter in the supermarkets. The selection is great nowadays. Be aware of buttermilk in the ingredients - that's not vegan. Our favourites are Flora and Naturli.

Pickled vegetables

It's always good to have a choice of some pickled vegetables in the fridge, especially gherkins and jalapenos.

Table sauces

They are simply handy to have to transform your meals, as they can be easily added to salad dressings, marinades, dips, etc.

We like to have a selection of mustards (Dijon, wholegrain, hot), ketchup, BBQ, various chilli sauces, vegan mayonnaise, and Sriracha.

Pastry

A great solution for making a quick lunch or dinner filled with delicious vegetables, i.e. tarts, rolls, pies. Some of the ready-made puffs and shortcrust pastry are vegan.

Vegan ice cream

There's a great selection of vegan ice cream available in every major supermarket nowadays from tubes to cones. Our number 1 choice is Booja Booja.

Frozen vegetables

Having a few bags of frozen vegetables will come very handy when you have had a busy day, and didn't have time to do the shopping and want to cook something quickly. Frozen vegetables can be used in soups, stews, stir-fries etc.

Herbalicious dried Herbs & Spices in our inventory

We feel having a good mix of dried herbs & spices in the kitchen really makes the difference when cooking at home, and this is something that can be built up over time so don't panic if you only have a small selection to start with. A well stocked and varied supply allows you to get creative, so don't be afraid to experiment by mixing things up a bit, it's a great way to get to know your herbs & spices and you will soon discover what works best for you and the meals you want to create.

Here is a list of the dried herbs/spices we have to hand. On top of these we will also use fresh herbs/spices which will either be picked straight from our garden on the day or purchased from our local fruit & veg stall.

Mixing it up

One of the things we love doing is getting unconventional and experimenting with our herbs & spices. Don't be afraid to look at a recipe and turn it upside down by using something completely different, you may just create something magical.

TIP - if you are going to experiment, start by just preparing one meal to make sure you are happy with what you have created & to minimise wasting food, you can then prepare on a larger scale knowing you have got it right.

Why whole herbs are better than powders

When preparing your meals think about using whole herbs over powdered herbs, there is nothing better than the magical aroma rising up out of a pestle

& mortar, grinding herbs releases that potent flavour and natural oils which can only intensify the meal you are creating. Ground spices lose their potency very quickly. If you grind or grate your own spices as you need them, you can extend the shelf life for much longer.

Here are our recommended herbs and spices that are good to have; build up your inventory slowly, as you progress on your cooking adventure.

Sweet & warming

- Cinnamon
- Clove
- Allspice
- Anise
- Star Anise
- Fennel
- Liquorice
- Vanilla
- Marjoram

Warming

- Nutmeg
- Caraway
- Dill

Aromatic

- Coriander
- Juniper
- Rose
- Cardamom
- Basil
- Eucalyptus

Earthy

- Cumin
- Nigella
- Parsley
- Oregano
- Sage

Citrusy

- Lemongrass
- Bay leaf
- Galangal
- Lemon Myrtle
- Kaffir Lime

Sweet and sour

- Sumac
- Tamarind
- Carob

Toasty

- Sesame
- Smoked paprika
- Sweet paprika

Sulphurous

- Garlic powder
- Onion powder
- Mustard seeds
- Curry leaf
- Asafoetida

Pungent and warming

- Black pepper
- Sichuan pepper
- Cayenne pepper
- Pink peppercorns
- Ground jalapeno
- Chilli
- Ginger
- Tarragon

Cooling

- Mint
- Lavender
- Chamomile
- Lemon balm

Floral

- Rosemary
- Thyme

Unique taste

- Saffron
- Poppy
- Celery seed
- Turmeric
- Fenugreek
- Safflower
- Sorrel

Salty

- Sea salt
- Himalayan salt
- Black salt 'Kala Namak'

Great mixed herbs & spices to have handy

- Zaatar
- Mixed herbs or Herbs de Provence
- Various Curry Powders
- Chinese 5 Spice mix
- Harissa Spice
- Jamaican Jerk seasoning
- Barbeque mix
- Ras El Hanout
- Fajita seasoning

Fresh Produce

Why fresh produce? First and foremost, fresh fruit and vegetables are very much an important part of a healthy diet. They contain essential vitamins, minerals, fiber, antioxidants and other nutrients that are essential for good health.

We feel very strongly about supporting our local fruit & veg stall, apart from building a friendly relationship with the guys that run the stall, one of the main benefits of purchasing fresh produce is that it is "fresher" fruit & vegetables begin to lose their nutrients 24hrs after being picked. Better quality soil and more sustainable farming practices typically mean better tasting, more nutritious produce which only adds to the magic when creating your meals.

Another amazing point is you can structure your meals around the seasons so cooking with fresh produce never really gets boring. Also buying local food helps support the local economy and it also benefits the environment.

Our Recommended Suppliers

We only recommend companies and suppliers that we use personally and are 100% happy with their products or services, as well as whose values are aligned with what we believe in.

BUYING IN BULK

Buying in bulk is much cheaper in the long run and the companies listed below offer products of amazing quality and represent high ethics and integrity.

Tree Harvest: https://www.tree-harvest.com/ - our top choice for everything organic: culinary herbs, spices, nuts, seeds, beans, legumes, seaweeds, natural sweeteners, dried fruits, grains, flour, oils, medicinal herbs, as well as essential oils and many other bits

Buy Wholefoods Online: https://www.buywholefoodsonline.co.uk/ - another choice for top cupboard supplies

Suma Cooperative: https://www.suma.coop/ - a wonderful vegetarian cooperative established in 1977; great prices for bulk orders; they have a great selection of not only dry goods but also fridge and freezer products, like berries, vegan burgers, plant-based milk; you need to call them to register or request a catalogue

MEDICINAL HERBS

Indigo Herbs: https://www.indigo-herbs.co.uk/ - a wonderful herbal supplier from Glastonbury offering fried herbs, powders, tinctures and supplements.

Wellness Alchemy: https://www.facebook.com/wellnessalchemyhub - it's Dominica's nutrition and herbal medicine practice, where you can get personalised advice and order fully tailored herbal blends

OTHER

The Earth Nectar: https://earthnectar.co.uk/ - the finest, organic, grade 1, Kashmiri Saffron supplier in the UK

Raw Sport: https://www.rawsport.com/ - unquestionably the top UK supplier of the purest, organic and certified heavy metal, pesticides and herbicides free, plant-based protein powders and supplements

Breakfasts

Crumpets with Smashed Avocado and Scrambled Tofu

Crumpets are a nice light alternative to bread/rolls, which can have a wide range of toppings. Here we used our scrambled tofu & smashed avocado which resulted in a simple yet tasty combination which can really be enjoyed at any time of the day.

EQUIPMENT

- Toaster

INGREDIENTS

Serves 2-4

- 4 crumpets
- Scrambled tofu (see page 47)
- Smashed avocado (see page 51)
- Handful of cherry tomatoes
- Vegan butter

PREPARATION

Prepare the smashed avocado
Prepare the scrambled tofu

METHOD

Toast the crumpets to your liking and be generous when spreading the butter. Take a good dollop of the smashed avocado and spread on top, then place two heaped tablespoons of the scrambled tofu on top and garnish with the cherry tomatoes.

USEFUL TIP

Feel free to experiment and use some of our other recipes as toppings ie - kimchi, hummus or even our mexican non carne.

Crumpets with Smashed Avocado & Scrambled Tofu

Breakfast Rolls

Every now and then we love to indulge in one of our breakfast rolls, they are both comforting and very satisfying. Naughty but not naughty, and certainly a good start if you are planning to have a lazy day.

EQUIPMENT

- Deep Frying Pan
- Griddle pan
- Mandoline

INGREDIENTS

Serves 2-4

- scrambled tofu (see page 47)
- turmeric sauerkraut (see page 68)
- smashed avocado (see page 51)
- 4 sourdough rolls (or rolls of your choice)
- 2 tbsp rapeseed Oil (or oil of your choice)
- vegan butter

For Carroton (vegan bacon alternative)

- 2 carrots
- Liquid Smoke
- Tamari Sauce
- 2 tsp smoked paprika
- Pinch of cracked black pepper

PREPARATION

You need to already have the turmeric sauerkraut pre made
Pre make the smashed avocado
Peel and cut the ends off the carrots then use the mandoline to cut them into thin strips (lengthwise)
Press the tofu to drain off any excess water

METHOD

Place the griddle pan over a medium heat and add the oil, when the oil has heated add the sliced carrots and cook for 2 minutes on each side. Drizzle with liquid smoke & tamari then sprinkle the black pepper and 1 teaspoon of the smoked paprika and cook for a further 1-2 minutes then turn the carrots and repeat. Once both sides have been coated, keep turning until you reach your desired crispiness.

Whilst the carrots are cooking you can start the scrambled tofu.
Heat the oil up in the pan over a medium heat. Add the onion and cook until soft, add the garlic and pour the plant based milk in and mix well.

Crumble the tofu into the pan and mix with the onion and garlic. Add the spice mix and nutritional yeast and stir in until well combined. Cook for 5 minutes stirring occasionally until the plant based milk has evaporated.

Butter the rolls (you can toast them if you prefer) and add a good spoonful of the smashed avocado, spread evenly then add a heaped spoonful of the scrambled tofu and finish by topping with the sliced carrots and turmeric sauerkraut. Serve and enjoy.

USEFUL TIP

If you are not a fan of turmeric sauerkraut you can always replace it with our kimchi which is equally as delicious.

Breakfast Rolls

English Breakfast Reinvented

Here we turn the traditional once naughty fry up into something rather special which is an ideal option to go for if you are looking for a lazy start to the weekend.

EQUIPMENT

- 1 Large frying pan
- 2 Medium frying pans
- Griddle pan
- Cast iron or heavy pot
- Baking tray

INGREDIENTS

Serves 3-4

- Scrambled Tofu (see page 47)
- Kimchi (see page 168)
- 4 stems of cherry vine tomatoes
- 1 tbsp olive oil

For the Mushrooms

- 6-8 large field mushrooms
- 2 tbsp olive oil
- 2 tbsp soy sauce
- 2 tsp garlic granules
- good pinch of cracked black pepper

For Carroton (vegan bacon alternative)

- 2 carrots
- Liquid Smoke
- Tamari Sauce
- 2 tsp smoked paprika
- Pinch of cracked black pepper

For the cheesy spinach

- 150g spinach
- 1 tsp olive oil
- 1 tbsp soy sauce
- 3 garlic cloves
- handful of vegan feta cubes

PREPARATION

Peel and cut the ends off the carrots then use the mandoline to cut them into thin strips (lengthwise)
Peel and finely chop the garlic cloves
The kimchi needs to be pre made

METHOD

Preheat the oven to 220°C/425°F/gas 7

Place the griddle pan over a medium heat and add the oil, when the oil has heated add the sliced carrots and cook for 2 minutes on each side. Drizzle with liquid smoke & tamari then sprinkle the black pepper and 1 teaspoon of the smoked paprika and cook for a further 1-2 minutes then turn the carrots and repeat. Once both sides have been coated, keep turning until you reach your desired crispiness.

Heat 2 tablespoons of olive oil in the large frying pan and add the mushrooms, cook for 2 minutes on each side (place the cast iron or heavy pot on top of the mushrooms to press them, this will release their water giving them a more "meaty" texture). Remove the cast iron or heavy pot and then add the 2 tablespoons of soy sauce, garlic granules and black pepper, turn the mushrooms to coat and cook for a further 4 minutes turning occasionally.

Place the vine tomatoes onto the baking tray and drizzle 1 tablespoon of olive oil over them, place on the middle shelf of the oven and cook for 15 minutes.

Whilst the tomatoes are cooking you can start the scrambled tofu.

Heat the oil up in the pan over a medium heat. Add the onion and cook until soft, add the garlic and pour the plant based milk in and mix well.

Crumble the tofu into the pan and mix with the onion and garlic. Add the spice mix and nutritional yeast and stir in until well combined. Cook for 5 minutes stirring occasionally until the plant based milk has evaporated.

Heat 1 teaspoon of olive oil in the medium pan on a medium heat and add the chopped garlic and fry for 2-3 minutes until it releases its aroma. Add spinach and soy sauce and wilt, stirring continuously. Once the spinach has wilted, remove from the heat and stir in the vegan feta cubes.

Plate everything and serve with some freshly toasted bread and sauces of your choice, Enjoy.

English Breakfast Reinvented

Gluten Free Banana Bread

There are many recipes for banana bread out there, but very few for those avoiding gluten. This recipe uses different types of flour that result in a perfectly balanced loaf which is both light and moist and full of flavor.

EQUIPMENT

- Loaf tin
- Large mixing bowl
- Mixing spoon/spatula
- Toothpick or knife (for testing the texture)

INGREDIENTS

Serves 10-12

- 1 tbsp psyllium husk
- 3 medium ripe bananas
- 1/4 cup unsalted almond butter (or sub other nut or seed butter)
- 3 tbsp melted coconut oil
- 1/2 cup coconut sugar (or sub organic brown sugar)
- 2-3 tbsp maple syrup (or sub agave nectar or coconut nectar)
- 1/2 tsp sea salt
- 3/4 cup unsweetened plant-based milk
- 1 tbsp baking powder
- 1 cup almond meal (ground from raw almonds)
- cup tapioca flour
- cup buckwheat flour
- cup brown rice flour
- cup potato starch
- 1 cup gluten-free oats
- 1/2 cup chopped raw walnuts

PREPARATION

Peel the bananas (slicing one of them in half lengthwise to be used later) Roughly chop the raw walnuts

METHOD

Preheat the oven to 180°C/350°F/gas 4

Line a loaf pan with parchment paper or lightly grease the pan.

Place the bananas in the mixing bowl and mash well with a fork, you want a smooth texture. Add the almond butter, coconut oil, coconut sugar, maple syrup, sea salt, and plant-based milk and mix in to combine all the ingredients.

Add the baking powder, almond meal, gluten-free flour blend, and gluten-free oats and stir well. Lastly add half of the walnuts and mix in well. Pour the mixture into the tin and smooth with a spoon/spatula. Top with the remaining sliced banana and walnuts.

Bake for roughly 1 hour 15 minutes. When done, the loaf should feel firm and be crackly and golden brown on top.

Using a toothpick or knife test the firmness of the bread, gently push it into the bread and it should come out clean (or with very few crumbs). Let the bread rest in the pan for 10 minutes, then carefully loosen the sides with a knife or pull up on the parchment paper to transfer to a cooling rack. Let it cool completely before cutting or it will be tender and tend to crumble.

USEFUL TIP

The banana bread can be covered and kept at room temperature for up to 3 days.
You can also slice and freeze for up to 1 month. It also tastes great toasted or grilled with some nice vegan butter.

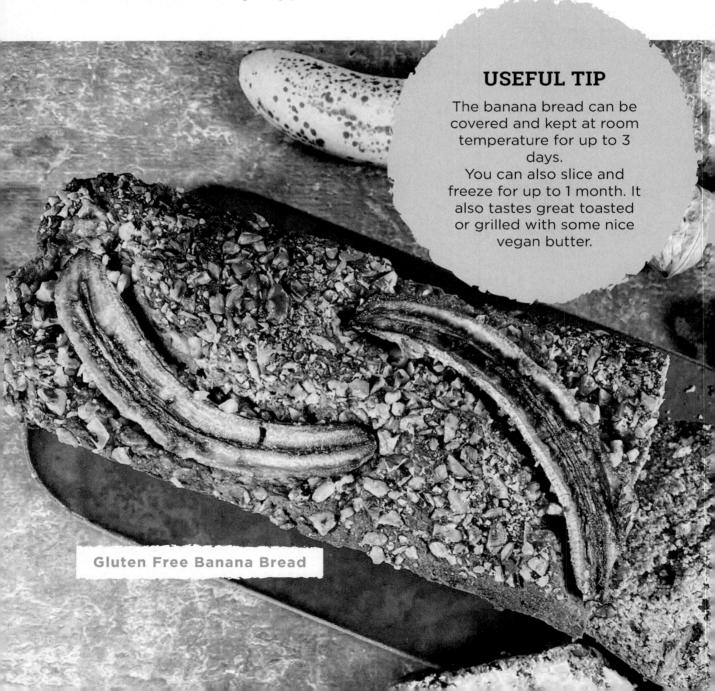

Gluten Free Banana Bread

Homemade Granola

We were looking for an alternative to granola that is refined sugar free, and this is what we came up with. Seeds and nuts are the source of beneficial fatty acids that should be enjoyed by everyone on a daily basis.

USEFUL TIP

Is absolutely delicious sprinkled over ice cream/yoghurt or on top of fruit salads.

EQUIPMENT

- Baking Tray
- Mixing Bowl

PREPARATION

Chop the dates
Roughly chop the nuts

INGREDIENTS

Makes roughly 30 portions

- 1/2 cup pumpkin seeds
- 1/2 cup sunflower seeds
- 3/4 mixed nuts
- 1/3 cup cacao nibs
- 2 cups puffed rice or quinoa
- 1 cup jumbo oats
- 1/2 cup flaxseed
- 1/2 cup coconut flakes
- 1/2 cup dates
- 1 cup mixed dried fruit (figs, dates, apricots)
- 2 heaped tbsp raw cacao powder (optional)
- 1 cup maple syrup
- 1 tbsp Cinnamon
- 2 tbsp burdock root powder
- 2 tbsp Siberian ginseng powder

METHOD

Preheat the oven to 170°C/325°F/gas 3

Place all the ingredients into a large mixing bowl and mix well. Scatter evenly across the baking tray and place on the middle shelf in the oven and bake for 30 minutes. Half way through take the baking tray out and using a spoon gently turn the mix. When the granola is ready, remove it from the oven and allow it to cool down completely before serving. You can also store it in an airtight container in a cool dark place for upto 3 months.

Homemade Granola

Hot Cinnamon Apple Porridge

Hot cinnamon and grated apple combined is an old tradition amongst Polish grandmas and served as a sweet treat. As it is so delicious it seemed only right to pair this with nutritious porridge to be enjoyed on cold mornings.

EQUIPMENT

- Small pot
- Medium pot
- Grater

INGREDIENTS

Serves 2-3

- 12 heaped tbsp rolled oats
- 2 glasses plant based milk
- 2 tsp maple syrup
- 2 sweet apples
- 2 tsp cinnamon
- 1 tbsp water

PREPARATION

Peel/core and grate the apples coarsely

METHOD

Add the plant based milk and rolled oats to a medium pot and place over a medium heat and bring to the boil, decrease the heat and let it simmer for 10 minutes or until you reach your desired texture. Add more milk if needed.

Put the apples into a small pot with 1 tablespoon of water and cook gently over a medium heat for 5 minutes. Add 1 teaspoon of cinnamon and 1 teaspoon of maple syrup, mix well and remove from the heat.

Put your cooked oats into a bowl and top with a generous spoonful of the cinnamon apples, you can dress with additional apple slices and walnuts.

USEFUL TIP

The grated apple and cinnamon also goes well served with rice pudding.

Hot Cinnamon Apple Porridge

Scrambled Tofu

This is our go to replacement for scrambled eggs, and it is in our opinion better than the real thing.

EQUIPMENT

• Medium Pan

INGREDIENTS

Serves 2-3

• 1tsp rapeseed oil
• 1/2 white onion
• 2 cloves garlic
• 1/3 tsp Indian black salt
• 1/2 tsp garlic granules (or powder)
• 1/2 tsp onion powder
• 1/2 tsp black pepper
• 1/4 tsp sea salt
• 2/3 tsp turmeric
• 2/3 tsp smoked paprika
• 120ml plant based milk
• 2 tbsp nutritional Yeast
• 396g firm or medium firm organic tofu

PREPARATION

Peel and finely chop the onion
Peel and mince the garlic
Mix all of the spices together apart from the nutritional yeast in a bowl
Press the tofu to remove any excess water

METHOD

Heat the oil up in the pan over a medium heat. Add the onion and cook until soft, add the garlic and pour the plant based milk in and mix well.

Crumble the tofu into the pan and mix with the onion and garlic. Add the spice mix and nutritional yeast and stir in until well combined. Cook for 5 minutes stirring occasionally until the plant based milk has evaporated. Serve and enjoy.

USEFUL TIP

This amazing scramble tofu can be enjoyed both cold and hot and can be added to many things ie - jacket potatoes, wraps, tarts, pizzas etc.

Scrambled Tofu

Seed & Nut Bread

Nutritionally packed delicious alternative to bread which supports your digestion, immune system, skin and cognition. All in all an extremely healthy experience that can be enjoyed every day.

EQUIPMENT

- Loaf tin
- Baking tray
- Large mixing bowl
- Spatula

INGREDIENTS

Serves 12-14

- ⅓ cup sunflower seeds
- ¼ cup pumpkin seeds
- ½ cup flaxseeds
- ¾ cup mixed nuts (almonds/ walnuts)
- 1 ½ cup rolled oats
- ½ cup dried cranberries
- 2 tbsp chia seeds
- 3 tbsp psyllium husk
- Pinch of salt
- 1 tbsp maple syrup
- 3 tbsp melted coconut oil
- 1 ½ cup water

PREPARATION

Roughly chop the nuts.

METHOD

Line the loaf tin with baking paper, mix all the ingredients together in the mixing bowl then transfer to the loaf tin. Set aside and cover with a tea towel for 1 hour.

After 30 minutes preheat the oven to 175°C/338°F/gas 4

Place the loaf tin on the middle shelf in the oven and back for 20 minutes. Remove the loaf tin from the oven and turn it upside down over the baking tray, gently lift the loaf tin and release the loaf, remove the baking paper and place the baking tray back into the oven and bake upside down for a further 40 minutes.

Remove from the oven and let it cool down completely before serving.

The loaf can be stored in an airtight container for upto 1 week.

Seed & Nut Bread

Smashed Avocado

This simple dish is a tasty delight that can be served with so many things and it is also extremely healthy. Avocado is one of the most nutrient-dense foods available, it is amongst the richest fruits and is high in fiber, folate, potassium, vitamin E & magnesium.

EQUIPMENT

- Mixing Bowl
- Juicer or manual citrus press

INGREDIENTS

Serves 2

- 2 avocados
- 1 lime (juiced)
- 1 red chilli or chilli flakes (optional)
- pinch of sea salt
- pinch of black pepper
- 1 tbsp nutritional yeast

PREPARATION

Juice the lime
Finely chop the chilli

METHOD

Halve the avocados and remove the seed, using a spoon scrape out the avocado and place in a bowl. Add the lime juice, chilli, pinch of sea salt & black pepper and the tablespoon of nutritional yeast. Gentle mash together using a fork until you get a smooth but slightly chunky texture.

Serve as an accompaniment and enjoy.

USEFUL TIP

Smashed avocado can be used in so many things: wraps, kebabs, pizza topping, jacket potatoes etc. You can also experiment with your smashed avocado by adding some chopped red onion or finely cubed tomatoes.

Smashed Avocado

Lunches & Dinners

Eastern European

"Green Alien" Superfoods Soup

This incredibly nutritious warming soup, rich in chlorophyll, iron and vitamin C that increases iron absorption. A great soup for anyone suffering from low energy, fatigue or anaemia.

EQUIPMENT

- Blender
- Medium pot

INGREDIENTS

Serves 3-4

- 1 broccoli
- 1 cup frozen green pea
- 2 cups spinach leaves
- 1 celery stick
- 1/2 bunch coriander
- 1 tbsp wheatgrass powder
- 1 tsp matcha tea powder
- 1 tsp sea salt
- 1 tsp black pepper
- 1.2 litre water
- 2 tsp vegetable stock powder
- 1 tsp thyme
- 1 tsp rosemary
- 1 tsp garlic powder
- 1 tsp onion powder

METHOD

Chop the celery into small cubes. Separate the broccoli florets and put them into the pot and pour over 1.2 l of water. Bring to a boil over a medium heat and then decrease the heat to a low and let it simmer until broccoli softens.

Add vegetable stock powder, frozen green pea, garlic powder, onion powder, rosemary, thyme, sea salt and black pepper. Cook for 10 more minutes.

Remove from the heat, stir in spinach leaves and let them wilt.

Add the soup to the blender along with the wheatgrass and matcha and whizz until smooth.

Serve in cups as a starter to your main or drink on its own on cold evenings.

'Green Alien' Superfood Soup

Buttery Cabbage

This traditional cabbage dish originates from Poland where it is served as an accompaniment to main meals.

USEFUL TIP

This lovely buttery cabbage can also be used to top pizzas, in wraps, in pies etc it can also be frozen and last upto 6 months.

EQUIPMENT

- Deep pan
- Small pan

INGREDIENTS

Serves 3-4

- 1 green cabbage
- 1 white onion
- 1 cup water
- 1/2 tsp cumin seeds
- 1tsp olive oil
- 1 tbsp oregano
- 1 heaped tsp black pepper
- 1/2 tsp sea salt

Roux mix
- 2 tbsp vegan butter
- 2 tbsp organic wheat flour

PREPARATION

Slice the onion and cabbage.

METHOD

Heat the olive oil in a deep pan and add the cumin seeds. Let them fry for a minute on a low heat so they can release their aroma but do not burn.

Add the sliced onion and fry until translucent. Add the chopped cabbage and pour 1 cup of water. Stir and let it slowly cook under cover on a medium heat for 20 minutes adding more water if needed, then add all the spices and cook until the cabbage is soft.

When the cabbage is almost ready, prepare the roux. Place the small pan on a low to medium heat and melt the butter, then add 2 tablespoons of flour and stir vigorously until well combined, remove from the heat and add to the cabbage while it is still cooking and mix well. Cook for another 2-3 minutes.

Buttery Cabbage

Chunky Vegetable Soup

Another traditional Polish soup that simply invites you to experiment with different vegetables to create a truly unique taste every single time.

EQUIPMENT

- Large pot

INGREDIENTS

Serves 6-8

- 1 red onion
- ½ leek
- 1 celery stick
- 1 carrot
- 1 parsnip
- ¼ celeriac
- 250g button mushrooms
- 350g white potatoes (approx. 3 medium)
- ½ romanesco
- ½ small cauliflower
- 2 sweet red peppers
- ¾ cup frozen pea
- 1 tbsp olive oil
- 1 tsp thyme
- 1 tsp marjoram
- 1 tbsp dark soy sauce
- 1 tsp sea salt
- 2 tsp sweet paprika
- 2 tbsp coconut yoghurt
- 1.5 litre vegetable stock

PREPARATION

Peel and cut the onion into big chunks.
Slice the leek and celery.
Cut carrot, celeriac and parsnip into medium size cubes.
Slice the mushrooms.
Peel and cube the potatoes.
Separate romanesco and cauliflower into florets.
Roughly cut red pepper into chunks.

METHOD

Pour the olive oil into a large pot and heat up on medium heat.

Add the onion, leek and celery and cook until softened.

Next, add the potatoes, carrot, celeriac, parsnip and mushrooms, and pour over the vegetable stock, cover and bring to a boil.

Add remaining vegetables: romanesco and cauliflower florets, red pepper and green pea, along with thyme, marjoram, sea salt, sweet paprika and soy sauce and reduce the heat to low, cover and simmer for 20-25 minutes or until the vegetables are soft. Add more water if necessary.

Remove from the heat and stir in the coconut yoghurt, serve and enjoy with a couple of slices of sourdough bread.

USEFUL TIP

This soup freezes well and can be stored for up to 6 months.

Chunky Vegetable Soup

Hungarian Sunshine

Being lovers of this traditional dish we just had to recreate it in our very own loving way, while keeping as much of the original recipe as we could.

EQUIPMENT

- Large pot

INGREDIENTS

Serves 4-6

- 300g button mushrooms
- 200g oyster mushrooms
- 100g soya chunks
- 500ml vegetable stock
- 1 tbsp soy sauce
- 2 tbsp barbeque seasoning
- 1 tbsp olive oil
- 2 onions
- 3 tomatoes
- 1 yellow bell pepper
- 3 sweet red peppers
- 4 garlic cloves
- 3 hot green chillies
- 1 ½ cup of water
- ⅓ cup soya yoghurt
- 2 tbsp nutritional yeast
- dill for garnishing

Spice mix
- 1 tsp cumin seeds
- 1 tsp onion granules
- 1 ½ tsp sea salt
- 1 tsp cracked black pepper
- 2 tbsp sweet paprika
- 1 tsp smoked paprika
- 2 bay leaves
- 3 tsp coconut sugar

PREPARATION

Mix both mushroom types and soya chunks in the airtight container and cover with vegetables stock, soya sauce and barbeque seasoning and marinate for a minimum of 3 hours.
Chop the onion, tomatoes and peppers into chunky cubes.
Mince the garlic.
Thinly chop green chillies.
Prepare your spice mix by putting all the ingredients into a bowl and mixing well.

METHOD

Add 1 tablespoon of olive oil into the deep pot and place over a medium heat, start with frying the onion for 2 minutes or until soft. Add the tomatoes, followed by your marinated mushrooms and soya chunks. Let tomatoes release their juices and then add red and yellow peppers, garlic and chillies. Pour 1 cup of water, add the spice mix and stir in.

Simmer on low heat for 20 minutes, and then stir in the yoghurt and nutritional yeast. Then remove from the heat.

Chop some dill to garnish and serve with mashed potatoes or sourdough bread.

Hungarian Sunshine

Polish "Bigos" (Cabbage Stew)

This is one of the most traditional eastern european dishes also known as "Hunter's Stew" consisting of different meats, but here we replace it with mushrooms and vegan sausages which once cooked if left to sit for longer the flavours just get better.

EQUIPMENT

- Large Pot
- Small Bowl

INGREDIENTS

Serves 8-10

- 2 white onions
- 4 garlic cloves
- 1 tbsp sea salt
- 1 tbsp cracked black pepper
- 1 white cabbage
- 1 cup turmeric sauerkraut (see page 68)
- 500g mixed mushrooms (chestnut & shiitake)
- 4-6 vegan sausages
- 300 hokkaido pumpkin
- ½ cup red lentils
- 1 tbsp wholegrain mustard
- 7 tbsp soya sauce
- 5-6 cups filtered water
- 1 tinned chopped tomatoes
- 10 prunes
- 2 tbsp tomato puree
- ½ cup red wine

Spice mix

- 2 tsp smoked paprika
- 1 tsp sweet paprika
- 1 tsp marjoram
- 6 bay leaves
- 8 cloves
- 2 tsp cumin seeds
- 1 tsp coriander seeds
- 1 tsp thyme
- ½ tsp allspice

PREPARATION

Add all the spice mix into a little bowl and mix well.

Chop the onion and mince garlic.

METHOD

Add 1 tablespoon of olive oil to a large pot and throw the chopped onion and minced garlic in and cook on low heat for 5 minutes. Next add 1 cup of sauerkraut and pour 2 cups of water. Cover and cook for another 20 minutes.

Meanwhile, cut the white cabbage in

half and then into quarters. Remove the hard bits and then slice into strips. Set aside.

Next peel and cube the pumpkin and peel/deseed then grate 1 apple.

Add all prepared ingredients (white cabbage, pumpkin and apple) to the pot and mix. Add 2 more cups of water and simmer on low for a few minutes.

Cut the prunes into quarters. Add them to the pot with your spice mix and the rest of the ingredients: red lentils, mustard, soya sauce, tinned tomatoes, red wine, and tomato puree, apart from the mushrooms and sausages. Cover and cook for around 2 hours on low heat.

Once the cabbage stew is ready, slice the mushrooms into chunky strips and fry until crispy. Season with salt and pepper, Set aside. Prepare vegan sausages as per instructions on the packaging and then slice. Add mushrooms and sausages to the cabbage stew and mix.

Serve with a knob of vegan butter and sourdough bread.

Polish 'Bigos' (Cabbage Stew)

Red Cabbage and Apple Salad

A truly exquisite, crunchy salad with a hint of maple syrup and hot red chilli.

EQUIPMENT

- Mandoline or sharp knife
- Grater
- Medium salad bowl

INGREDIENTS

Serves 2-3

- 1 small red cabbage
- 3 red sweet apples
- 1/2 tsp sea salt
- 1 tsp cracked black pepper
- 1 tsp dried marjoram
- 1 lemon
- 1 fresh chilli pepper
- 1 tbsp maple syrup
- 2 tbsp extra virgin olive oil

METHOD

Put the cabbage and apple into a bowl and add all the seasoning ingredients. Massage them into the cabbage and leave for 10 minutes to let the cabbage release its juices. Mix once again and serve.

PREPARATION

Cut the red cabbage in quarters, remove the core and slice thinly into strips using mandoline or a sharp knife.
Peel, core and coarsely grate the apples.
Juice the lemon.

Red Cabbage & Apple Salad

Turmeric Sauerkraut

An exotic twist to a traditional sauerkraut.

EQUIPMENT

- Mandoline or sharp knife
- Large Bowl
- Large glass airtight jar

INGREDIENTS

Makes around 2 litres

- 1 medium white cabbage
- 2 tbsp sea salt
- 2 tsp caraway seeds
- 2 tsp turmeric
- pinch of saffron

METHOD

Remove the outer leaves from the cabbage then cut the cabbage into quarters and remove the hard ends and set them to the side. Using a mandoline or sharp knife, slice thinly and transfer to the large bowl. Sprinkle with the sea salt and massage until the cabbage gets softer and starts to release its juices.

Add the remaining spices and mix well, then transfer to the large glass airtight jar, leaving approximately 2 inches from the top. Press the cabbage down into the jar and place the leaves you removed on top along with the hard ends (this is to stop the cabbage from rising as it ferments) add additional water (must be filtered or boiled and cooled) to cover the cabbage entirely leaving no more than 1 inch from the top. Close the jar and store in a cool dry place and leave to ferment for 4 weeks.

Every day during the 1st week of fermenting it is important to check daily and slightly open the jar to release any build up of pressure. The following weeks repeat this step every 3-4 days until ready.

Once ready, store in the fridge for upto 3 months.

USEFUL TIP

This beautiful sauerkraut can be used as an accompaniment to so many things, try adding to wraps, sandwiches, pizza topping etc

Turmeric Sauerkraut

Ukrainian Borscht with a Twist

In Eastern Europe, there are many different variations of Borscht and this is our version with a twist.

EQUIPMENT

- Large pot
- Grater

INGREDIENTS

Serves 3-4

- 4 cloves garlic
- 1 large white onion
- 1 tbsp olive oil
- 2 beetroots
- 1 carrot
- 1/2 small white cabbage
- 3 potatoes approx. 350g
- 2l vegetable stock
- 1 tbsp tomato puree
- 1 tin chopped tomatoes
- 1/2 cup frozen pea
- 2 tomatoes
- 1 tsp sea salt
- 2 tsp black pepper
- 3 tbsp white wine vinegar
- 3 bay leaves
- 1 tsp brown sugar
- 1 tsp allspice, ground
- 2 tbsp Nutritional Yeast
- 5 tbsp kimchi plus additional for serving (see page 168)
- A few vegan feta cubes
- A small handful of fresh parsley or coriander
- Cashew sour cream for topping (see page 192)

PREPARATION

Kimchi needs to be premade.
Peel and slice the garlic cloves
Peel, halve & slice the onion.
Quarter the tomatoes.
Chop the coriander or parsley.
Chop the beetroots into small cubes.
Chop potatoes into chunky cubes
Grate the cabbage.
Grate the carrots.

METHOD

Add 1 tablespoon of olive oil into the pot and place over low heat. Let the garlic and onion slowly cook until soft.

Add the beetroot, potatoes, cabbage & carrots to the pot and mix thoroughly with the onion and garlic.

Pour 2 litres of vegetable stock into the pot and add the chopped tinned tomatoes and bay leaves.

Simmer on low to medium heat for around 15 minutes.

Add the frozen green peas, vinegar, brown sugar, allspice, marjoram, coriander or parsley, sea salt, black pepper, onion granules, garlic granules and tomato puree. Follow by adding quartered fresh tomatoes and 5 tablespoons of kimchi.

Simmer for another 20 minutes and then add nutritional yeast, half of the vegan feta cubes and stir until well mixed in.

Serve with chopped coriander or parsley, a spoonful of kimchi, cashew sour cream and a few feta cubes, enjoy.

Ukrainian Borscht with a Twist

Indian

Beetroot and Paneer Style Red Curry

This wonderful dish is a result of our interpretation of how beetroot and extra firm tofu could be combined to create the most delicious curry bursting with earthly flavours.

EQUIPMENT

- Small pot
- Medium pan
- Tofu press (optional)

INGREDIENTS

Serves 3-4

- 4 medium raw beetroots
- 1 tbsp olive oil
- 1 red onion
- 3 cloves garlic
- 1 tin butter beans
- 1 bunch of chard (or use beetroot leaves)
- 1 cup water
- 3/4 cup oat milk
- 170g extra firm tofu
- 1 apple
- 1tbsp maple syrup
- 1 tbsp tomato puree
- 1 tbsp nutritional yeast
- 1/2 tsp black pepper
- pinch of salt

For the spice mix
- 1 aniseed
- 1/2 tsp cumin seeds
- 1/2 tsp fenugreek seeds
- 1/2 tsp nutmeg
- 1 tsp turmeric

PREPARATION

Cut the beetroot leaves and stems off and boil the beetroots with the skin on for 30 mins or until medium soft in a small pot. Check the firmness with a fork. Once ready, let them cool down, then peel and chop into small cubes.

Peel and chop red onion.
Peel and mince the garlic.
Roughly chop chard leaves (or beetroot leaves) including stems.
Press the tofu to remove excess water and cut it into cubes.
Peel, core and cube the apple.
Mix your spices in a small bowl and set to the side.

METHOD

Heat the olive oil in a medium pan on a medium heat and add your spice mix, cook until they release their aroma. Reduce to low heat and add the onion, cook until softened, stirring frequently to coat it in spices.

Add the garlic followed by beetroot, butter beans, chopped chard and apple and pour 1 cup of water in. Increase the heat back to medium, cover and simmer for 10 minutes stirring from time to time.

Next, add the oat milk, maple syrup, tomato puree, a pinch of salt, black pepper, tofu cubes and nutritional yeast. Mix well to combine, cover and simmer for an additional 10 minutes, stirring frequently to prevent the ingredients from sticking to the bottom of the pan.

Serve hot with Coriander, Lime & Saffron Rice (see page 78). Enjoy!

USEFUL TIP

The surplus of this unusual Indian dish is absolutely delicious in wraps that you can enjoy as a light lunch the next day.

Beetroot & Paneer Style Red Curry

Chickpea and Spinach Flatbread

This delightfully delicious spinach flatbread is versatile and by simply changing some of the spices it can be served as an accompaniment to many different dishes.

EQUIPMENT

- Blender or whisk
- Large mixing bowl
- Non-stick medium frying pan

INGREDIENTS

Serves 3-4

- 1 big handful spinach
- 100g gram flour
- pinch sea salt
- splash olive oil
- 1 tsp turmeric
- 1 tsp cumin seeds
- 1 tsp apple cider vinegar
- 200ml water

PREPARATION

Roughly chop the spinach

METHOD

Add the gram flour and seasoning to a large bowl and stir well to combine.

Add in the water, olive oil, spinach and vinegar. Mix to a smooth batter. Set aside for 10 minutes.

Add a little oil to the base of a non-stick medium frying pan. Add 1/4 cup of the batter to the pan and swirl around the bottom to create the shape of the bread.

Cook on a medium heat for approximately 2 minutes until there are bubbles in the bread and you can lift it over to flip it easily. Flip and cook on the other side for 30 seconds to a minute.

Remove from the pan and place on a plate and cover with a clean cloth to keep warm. Repeat the process with the remaining batter.

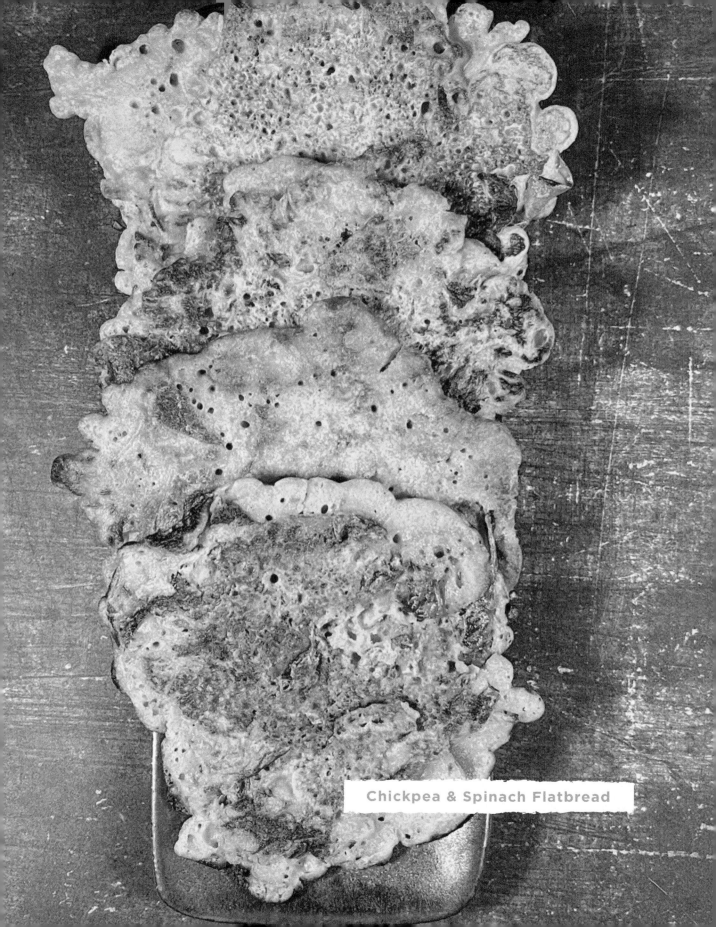

Chickpea & Spinach Flatbread

Coriander Lime & Saffron Rice

Coriander and lime are a match made in heaven and these simple ingredients make a simple rice dish truly exceptional. Saffron adds not only the colour, but its unique sweet floral taste, while the butter makes it creamy.

EQUIPMENT

- Medium pot
- Pestle and mortar

INGREDIENTS

Serves 2-4

- 250g basmati rice
- 1 lime
- 1 tbsp vegan butter
- pinch of organic saffron
- 1 bunch of coriander
- 1/2 tsp sea salt

METHOD

Boil the basmati rice as per the instructions on the package.

Crush the saffron threads in a pestle and mortar then transfer to a small bowl and cover with 2 tbsp boiling water. Set to the side.

Roughly chop the coriander and once the rice is ready, mix it with vegan butter, sea salt, coriander, saffron (use the infused water as well), squeeze the lime over the rice and mix well to combine.

Serve hot with your favourite dishes.

Cream of Roasted Tomato, Parsnip and Red Lentil

A perfect wholesome soup to warm the soul on those chilly evenings.

EQUIPMENT

- Blender
- Baking tray
- Medium pot

INGREDIENTS

Serves 3-4

- 6 sweet tomatoes (i.e. san marzano)
- 1 parsnip
- 2 shallots
- 4 cloves garlic
- 1/2 cup red split lentils
- salt to taste
- black pepper to taste
- 1/4 tsp cayenne pepper
- 1/2 tsp turmeric
- drizzle of olive oil
- boil 1/2 cup red split lentils.

METHOD

Preheat the oven to 220°C/425°F/gas 7

Place all the vegetables on the baking tray, drizzle with olive oil and place on the middle shelf of the oven and bake for 25 minutes.

Once done place the roasted vegetables into the blender along with cooked lentils adding more water as you blend to achieve your desired texture. Once you have achieved your desired texture pour the contents into the pot and place over a medium heat.

Add the spices and bring to the boil. Once boiled, decrease the heat and simmer for 5 minutes.

Serve with a dollop of plant based yoghurt and sprouted seeds.

PREPARATION

Cut the tomatoes in half
Peel and slice the parsnip
Peel and cut the shallots in half
Peel the garlic

Cream of Roasted Tomato, Parsnip & Red Lentil

Cucumber & mint raita

A simple yet tasty accompaniment which serves as a cooling side dish to any hot curries.

EQUIPMENT

- Grater
- 2 medium mixing bowls

INGREDIENTS

Serves 2-3 as a side

- 1/2 cucumber
- 2 tbsp fresh mint
- pinch of sea salt
- 1 tsp cracked black pepper
- 1 small lime
- plant-based yoghurt

METHOD

Grate the cucumber and place it into a bowl, sprinkle it with sea salt and set aside.
Meanwhile, chop the fresh mint and add it to the 2nd bowl, squeeze the lime in and mix with the yoghurt and black pepper.

Squeeze the excess water from the cucumber and place it in the 2nd bowl and mix with the yoghurt and mint.

Cucumber & Mint Raita

Curried Cabbage

Polish tradition meets Indian tradition in this simply scrumptious side dish.

EQUIPMENT

- Frying pan
- Small pan
- Sharp knife

INGREDIENTS

Serves 2-3

- 1 savoy cabbage
- 1 white onion
- 4 garlic cloves
- 1 tbsp olive oil
- pinch of sea salt
- 1 tsp black pepper

Spice mix
- 1 tsp fennel seeds
- 1 tsp cumin seeds
- 2 tsp turmeric

For the Roux
- 2 heaped tbsp butter
- 1 level tbsp plain flour

PREPARATION

Cut the cabbage into quarters and remove the hard ends, slice into chunky strips.
Peel and chop the onion into small cubes.
Peel and mince the garlic.

METHOD

Preheat the oil in the pan and add fennel and cumin seeds and allow the aromas to release.

Add the chopped onion and fry until softened.

Add the sliced cabbage to the pan along with the chopped garlic and mix. Pour 1 cup of water and cover with the lid. Cook for 15 minutes on medium heat or until the cabbage is soft.

Add the turmeric, sea salt and black pepper half way through.

Melt the butter in the small pan. Add the flour and mix thoroughly until there are no lumps.

Mix in with cabbage and cook for 5 minutes.

Curried Cabbage

Curry Pizza

We like to cook outside of the box and are always mixing cuisines to see what we can come up with. The birth of this simply stunning pizza is a prime example of getting creative with surplus food from a previously cooked meal. We are pleased to introduce you to our Sweet Potato, Green Pea & Mint curry pizza.

EQUIPMENT

- Pizza tray
- Blender

INGREDIENTS

For the Base
- Sourdough pizza base (we use M&S pizza bases) or you can make your own or use one of your choice.

For the Base sauce
- Hot Aromatic Green Sauce (see page 196)

Toppings
- Handful of Baby Spinach leaves
- Sweet potato, Green pea & Mint curry (see page 94)
- Crumbled Feta (we use M&S Plant Kitchen Feta)

METHOD

Preheat the oven to 220°C/425°F/gas 7

Place the pizza base onto a pizza tray and give the base a generous coat of the Hot Aromatic Green Sauce, next scatter the baby spinach leaves on top, Now evenly spoon the sweet potato, green pea & mint curry over the top and finish by crumbling the feta cubes making sure you cover evenly. Place on the middle shelf of the oven and cook for 10-12 minutes.

Serve with any sides of your choice and enjoy.

Curry Pizza

Earthy Green Lentil & Spinach Dhal

This earthy green lentil & spinach dhal resembles the grounding flavours of mother nature. An absolute must have on those cold evenings.

EQUIPMENT

- Food Processor or Blender
- Large frying pan

INGREDIENTS

Serves 4-6

- 1 onion
- 1 tbsp olive oil
- 3 cloves garlic
- 200 g green lentils rinsed
- 750ml water
- 200g spinach
- 3 tbsp coconut yoghurt or cream
- 1 tsp sea salt
- 1/2 tsp black pepper

Spice mix
- 1 tsp black mustard seeds
- 1 tsp turmeric
- 1 tsp cumin seeds
- 1 tsp ground coriander
- 1/2 tsp chilli flakes
- 4 bay leaves

PREPARATION

Peel and roughly chop the onion. Peel and slice the garlic.

METHOD

Firstly add the oil to a large frying pan and place over a medium heat. Add in the mustard seeds and When they start to pop add in the cumin seeds, coriander, turmeric, bay leaves and chilli flakes and stir for a few seconds then add the onion.

Fry for approx 8-10 minutes on a low heat until soft and browning. Add in the garlic and stir for another few minutes. Now add the lentils and water. Simmer for 25 minutes stirring occasionally. Add more water if needed.

Blitz the spinach with 2 tablespoons of water in a food processor or blender until roughly chopped up, now add the spinach to the pan and simmer for a further 5 minutes.

Stir in the plant based yoghurt, salt and black pepper.

Top with more yoghurt and serve.

Earthy Green Lentil & Spinach Dhal

Hot Chickpea & Cauliflower Curry

We love to create our own dishes and this stunning infusion of Indian spices blended beautifully with the chickpeas & cauliflower.

EQUIPMENT

- Large pan with lid

INGREDIENTS

Serves 3-4

- 1 white onion
- 3 cloves garlic
- 2 large tomatoes
- 1 tin chickpea
- 1/2 cauliflower
- 1 tsp turmeric
- 1/2 tsp garam masala
- 1/2 tsp cayenne pepper
- 1/2 tsp cracked black pepper
- pinch of salt
- 1/2 cup filtered water
- 1 tin coconut milk
- 1 handful fresh coriander
- 1/2 lime
- 1 tbsp olive oil

Spice seeds mix
- 1 tsp mustard seeds
- 1/2 tsp fennel seeds
- 1/2 tsp cumin seeds
- 1 tsp coriander seeds
- 1/2 tsp fenugreek

PREPARATION

Peel and chop the onion into chunky cubes.
Quarter the tomatoes.
Cut the cauliflower into small florets.
Roughly chop the coriander.
Juice the lime.

METHOD

Pour the olive oil in the pan and heat up over a medium heat. Add your seeds and let them release their aroma, be careful not to burn them.

Add the chunky white onion and fry until soft. Add tomatoes, chickpea and cauliflower florets. Mix with turmeric, garam masala, cayenne and half a cup of water. Cook under the lid for 10 minutes.

When the cauliflower gets softened, add the coconut milk, salt and pepper. Cover with lid and simmer on low for an additional 10 minutes.

Stir in the fresh coriander and lime juice.

Serve and enjoy.

Hot Chickpea & Cauliflower Curry

Quick Red Lentil Dhal

Absolutely delicious nutritious filling dhal that can be prepared in less than 30 minutes.

EQUIPMENT

- Large Pan
- Grater
- Pestle & Mortar

INGREDIENTS

Serves 3-4

- 1 cup red lentils
- 3 cups vegetable stock
- 1 tbsp olive oil
- 1/2 tsp cumin seeds
- 1/2 tsp fennel seeds
- 1/2 tsp coriander seeds
- 1/2 tsp mustard seeds
- 1/2 tsp cardamom powder
- 1 tsp turmeric
- 1 tsp sweet paprika
- 1 inch fresh ginger
- 1 red chilli (optional)
- 3 cloves garlic
- 1 white onion
- 2 tomatoes
- 1 lemon
- 100g spinach

PREPARATION

Peel and finely chop the onion.
Finely chop the tomatoes.
Peel and grate the ginger.
Grind the cumin, fennel, coriander and mustard seeds lightly in a pestle and mortar.
Juice the lemon.

METHOD

Heat the oil in a large pan over a medium heat. Add the chopped onion and cook gently for 5 minutes. Then add the garlic, ginger and red chilli and cook for a further 2 - 3 minutes.

Add the cumin, fennel, coriander and mustard seeds to the pan, along with the turmeric, sweet paprika and cardamom and cook for 1 minute.

Add the lentils, chopped tomatoes and vegetable stock, then stir in to combine. Season with salt and pepper and cook on a medium heat for 15-20 minutes until reduced and thick.

If you have time, you can leave it a

little longer on a very low heat for even more flavour (just stir often and check it doesn't scorch on the bottom of the pan).

Taste and add more chilli if desired.

Stir in the lemon juice and spinach until it wilts.

Serve and enjoy.

Quick Red Lentil Dhal

Sweet Potato, Green Pea, Mint & Coconut Curry

This dish was simply an experiment that turned out to be an absolutely divine dish with an explosion of flavours.

EQUIPMENT

- Deep Pan

INGREDIENTS

Serves 4-6

- 1 large sweet potato
- 1 cup frozen green pea
- 1 bunch mint
- 1 tin coconut milk
- 1 tbsp garam masala mix
- 2 tsp turmeric
- 1 tsp fenugreek
- 1 tsp ground ginger
- 1/2 tsp nutmeg
- 1/4 tsp chilli powder
- 1 tsp black pepper
- pinch of salt
- 1 cup water

PREPARATION

Peel and chop the sweet potato into small cubes.
Roughly chop the mint.

METHOD

Heat the oil in the pan and add the fenugreek seeds, lightly cook until they release their aroma and then add the sweet potato, Pour 1 cup of water and stir. Cover with the lid and simmer on medium heat for 5-7 minutes or until the potatoes start getting softer.

Add the green pea, garam masala, turmeric, ginger and nutmeg, stir well and cook for 2 more minutes.

Add the coconut milk (only the creamy bit, discard the water), mint, pinch of salt, black pepper and chilli. Simmer gently for another 5 minutes.

Serve and enjoy

Sweet Potato, Green Pea, Mint & Coconut Curry

Tandoori Masala Mushroom Curry

If you are a lover of mushrooms, this simple yet delicious dish is a must try.

EQUIPMENT

- Potato masher
- Deep pan
- Large airtight container

INGREDIENTS

Serves 3-4

- 600g field mushroom
- 2 tsp dark soy sauce
- handful of fresh coriander
- 1 large onion
- 2 tbsp olive oil

For the Tandoori Masala spice mix (or you can use a pre made Tandoori mix)

- coriander (dried)
- paprika
- salt
- garlic granules
- chilli powder
- cumin powder
- fenugreek powder
- onion powder
- celery powder
- ginger powder
- cinnamon
- cloves
- star aniseed
- fennel
- black pepper
- lemon zest
- bay leaves (dried & finely chopped)
- nutmeg powder

For the Chunky Tomato sauce

- 830g vine tomatoes
- 1 tin plum tomatoes
- 1 tsp sea salt
- 1 tsp cracked black pepper
- 1 tbsp of mixed herbs
- 1 tsp garlic granules
- 1 tsp onion granules

PREPARATION

Cube the mushrooms.
Chop the coriander.
Peel/halve & quarter the onion (separate the pieces).

If you are making the tandori masala spice mix, use a pestle & mortar to grind the bay leaves, cloves, star aniseed & fennel then along with the rest of the spice mix ingredients add them to a bowl and mix them all together.

Dice the vine tomatoes into chunky cubes.

METHOD

Add the mushrooms, dark soy sauce, tandoori masala spice mix & coriander into an airtight container, put the lid on and shake well until the mushrooms are well coated then place in the fridge for 1hr to marinade (shake every 20 minutes).

Whilst waiting for the mushrooms to marinade, take the ingredients for the chunky tomato sauce and add to a large bowl, mix well using a spoon then take a potato masher and gently mash the contents until the tomatoes break up and release some juice, give it a stir and set to the side.

Once the mushrooms have marinaded, take a deep frying pan and place over a medium/high heat, add 2 tablespoons of olive oil and when the oil is hot add the marinated mushrooms and cook for 5 minutes stirring occasionally. Add the quartered onion and stir in to coat in the marinade and cook for a further

3 minutes, stirring occasionally. Finally add the chunky tomato sauce and stir for a minute to make sure everything is mixed well, reduce the heat to a small flame and place the lid on the frying pan, continue to cook for another 20 minutes making sure to stir every 5 minutes.

Serve and enjoy.

USEFUL TIP
The marinated mushrooms can also be used in a number of ways, we use them to create some other fantastic dishes like pizza, pies, tarts, wraps etc

Tandoori Masala Mushroom Curry

Tandoori Masala Mushroom Slice

Being lovers of pastry, we are always looking to see what we can use as fillers and this delight was created using some surplus from one of our curry nights.

EQUIPMENT

- Baking tray
- Baking Paper
- Basting brush
- Medium pan

INGREDIENTS

Serves 2-3

- ready rolled puff pastry
- tandoori masala mushrooms (see page 96)
- small handful of chopped coriander
- oat milk (to brush pastry)

METHOD

Preheat the oven to 220°C/425°F/gas 7

Reheat the Tandoori Masala Mushrooms in a pan over a medium heat (surplus from the Indian meal you cooked) or make from scratch (see page 96), once the mushrooms are ready remove from the gas and set to the side.

Roll out the puff pastry and divide into two even halves, place a sheet of baking paper on the oven tray and lay one half of the puff pastry down, carefully spoon the tandoori masala mushrooms over the puff pastry spreading evenly.

Lay the other half of the puff pastry over the top and push the edges down to seal the pastry slice, then turn the edges back on themselves to create a fold and gently press down using a fork.

Gently score the top of the pastry slice but do not cut through the pastry, using a brush gently coat the pastry with the oat milk (this adds the crispiness to the pastry). Place the baking tray into the middle of the oven and cook for 15-25 minutes or until the pastry has developed a golden brown colour. Once cooked, sprinkle a little chopped coriander over the top and serve on its own or with sides of your choice, Here we have served with our Mango Lime & Chilli ketchup (see page 198), Enjoy.

Tandoori Masala Mushroom Slice

Tandoori Style Raw Vegan Lasagna

Courgette slices serve as a wonderful replacement for the lasagna sheets in raw vegan dishes. They are crunchy, have the perfect texture and beautiful taste. Here we married an Italian idea with Indian spices and the effect is simply: WOW!

Deep flavour tandoori mushrooms balanced by rich tomato sauce and turmeric cheese sauce with a strong hint of coriander, chilli and lime pesto. Flavours dancing together in your mouth!

EQUIPMENT

- Food processor
- Blender
- Mixing bowl
- Mandoline
- Potato masher

INGREDIENTS

Serves 4

- 4 green courgettes

For Tandoori mushrooms

- 5 or 6 portobello mushrooms
- 2 -3 tbsp tandoori seasoning
- Handful of Coriander
- 2 tbsp soy sauce

For the red sauce

- 760g vine tomatoes
- 50g sundried tomatoes
- 1 tbsp miso paste
- 3 garlic cloves
- 1 tsp onion granules
- 1 tbsp mixed herbs
- 2 tsp soy sauce
- 1 tsp crushed chilli (optional)
- pinch of psyllium husk
- cracked black pepper, to taste
- sea salt, to taste

For the curry cream

- 1 cup cashews
- 1 heaped tsp turmeric
- 1/4 tsp asafoetida
- 1 lemon
- 1 tbsp garlic granules
- 1 shallot onion
- 1/3 cup nutritional yeast
- 1/4 tsp sea salt
- black pepper, to taste
- 1/4 cup plant-based milk

For the green sauce

- 1 bunch coriander
- 1 small bunch mint
- 2.5" fresh ginger (grated)
- 4 garlic cloves
- 2 limes
- 1 fresh hot red chilli
- 1/2 tsp sea salt
- 1/2 tsp black pepper
- 1/2 cup pumpkin seeds

PREPARATION

Cut the portobello mushrooms into chunky cubes and place in the airtight container along with the soy sauce, tandoori seasoning, chopped coriander and marinate for a minimum of 5 hours

Chop the vine tomatoes
Soak the sun-dried tomatoes in boiling water for 30 mins.
Peel and mince the garlic.

Soak the cashews in boiling water for 30 minutes.
Juice the lemon.

Roughly chop the coriander and mint.
Peel and finely grate the ginger.
Peel and mince the garlic.
Juice the limes.
Deseed and finely chop the red hot chilli.

METHOD

Prepare the sauces first. For the red sauce, start with gently mashing the chopped vine tomatoes and then mix with minced garlic, mixed herbs, sea salt, black pepper, onion granules, chilli and soy sauce. Strain the soaked sundried tomatoes, and blend with miso and some of the juice released by the mashed vine tomatoes. Once ready, mix with the rest of the tomatoes and set to the side.

For the curry cream, strain the cashews and blend with all the ingredients until very smooth. Transfer into a container or a bowl and set aside.

Put all the green sauce ingredients into the food processor and process until you get a creamy texture. Set aside.

Cut the courgette lengthwise on the mandoline into 0.5cm strips. One portion equals 1 courgette.

Place 3 strips of courgette on a plate and top up with the red sauce and drizzle with the cheesy curry cream. Place another 3 strips of courgette on top and lay the marinated tandoori mushrooms. Lay another 3 strips of courgette on top of the mushroom, top with the green sauce, more courgette and a generous amount of yellow cheesy cream.

Enjoy!

Tandoori Style Raw Vegan Lasagna

Mediterranean

Brussel Sprout & Caramelised Red Onion Paccheri

Taking inspiration from the traditional cannelloni we wanted to create something which was slightly different in style but oozing in flavour.

EQUIPMENT

- Medium oven dish
- Large oven dish
- Medium pan
- Large Bowl
- Grater
- Potato masher
- Piping bag or small spoon
- Tin Foil

INGREDIENTS

Serves 4-6

- 40 x single grain pache pasta tubes

For the Brussels
- 30 brussel sprouts
- Glug of olive oil
- 2 tbsp maple syrup
- 1 tsp sea salt
- 1 tsp cracked black pepper

For the Caramelised Red Onion
- 1.5 tbsp olive oil
- 2 red onion
- 2 tbsp coconut sugar
- 1 tsp sea salt

For the Chunky Tomato Sauce
- 5 vine tomatoes
- 1 tin of italian plum tomatoes
- 1.5 tsp onion granules
- 2 tsp garlic granules
- 1 tbsp italian seasoning
- 1 heaped tsp smoked paprika
- 2 tsp chilli flakes (optional)
- Salt & pepper to taste

For the toppings
- fresh basil
- lemon zest
- vegan feta

PREPARATION

Trim the ends and remove any discoloured leaves from the brussels. Peel and finely chop the red onion. Roughly chop the vine tomatoes. Grate the lemon and put the zest to the side.

METHOD

Preheat the oven to 200°C/400°F/gas 6

For the roast Brussel Sprouts

Use a medium sized ceramic oven dish and cover the bottom with a good glug of olive oil, add 2 tablespoons of maple syrup and a good pinch of salt & pepper to taste, mix well with a fork.

Place the brussels in the oven dish and shake gently until they are all covered in the oil mix (we massage each brussel to ensure they are all coated). Cover the oven dish with foil and place in the middle of the oven and cook for 25 minutes, remove the foil and check they are soft to the touch, cook for further 5 minutes to add some crisp to the outer shell, once done set to the side.

In a pan over a medium heat add 1.5 tablespoons of olive oil, add the red onions, 1 teaspoon of salt and cook until the onions are translucent and soft, then add 2 tablespoons of coconut sugar and stir in and cook until they are caramelised.
.
Add the roasted brussels and the caramelised red onion to a large bowl and use a potato masher to mash and mix them together (you can also chop if needed). Once done, put to the side.

For the chunky Tomato base

In a large bowl add the vine tomatoes, tin of Italian plum tomatoes, 1.5 teaspoons of onion granules, 2 teaspoons of garlic granules, 1 tablespoon of Italian seasoning, 1 heaped teaspoon of smoked paprika, salt & pepper to taste and finally 2 teaspoons of crushed chilli flakes (optional) now mash the contents with a potato masher to release the juices and mix well.

Add the chunky tomato sauce to the large sized oven dish and spread evenly.

Now take the brussels & caramelised onion mix and fill the Paccheri tubes (you can use a piping bag or small spoon) then sit them in the tomato sauce facing upwards in even rows.

Crumble some of the vegan feta cheese over the top, cover the oven dish with foil and return it to the middle shelf and cook for 25 minutes, then remove the foil and cook for a further 10 minutes.

Once cooked, remove from the oven and crumble some more of the vegan feta over the top, sprinkle with the grated lemon zest and finish with fresh basil, serve and enjoy.

USEFUL TIP
If you have surplus brussel mix/tomato sauce you can reuse them in many different ways - pizza base/ topping, sandwich fillers, toast toppers etc

Brussel Sprout & Caramelised Red Onion Paccheri

Chunky Tomato Supreme Pizza

If you are looking for something super quick and simply scrumptious then our home made pizzas are a must try.

EQUIPMENT

- Pizza tray
- Frying pan

INGREDIENTS

Serves 1-3

- sourdough pizza base (we use M&S pizza base) or you can make your own or choose one of your choice.
- 1 tbsp olive oil

For the chunky tomato base sauce
- 5 large sized vine tomatoes
- 1 x tin of italian plum tomatoes
- 1.5 tsp of onion granules
- 2 tsp of garlic granules
- 1 tbsp of italian seasoning
- 1 heaped tsp of smoked paprika
- pinch of sea salt & pepper to taste
- 2 tsp of crushed chilli flakes (optional)

For the Toppings
- handful of spinach
- 1 yellow pepper (de seeded & sliced)
- 1 red onion (peeled & sliced)
- 3-4 mushrooms (sliced)
- handful of jalapenos

METHOD

Preheat the oven to 220°C/425°F/gas 7.

Dice the vine tomatoes and put them In a large bowl, add the tin of Italian plum tomatoes, onion granules, garlic granules, Italian seasoning, smoked paprika, salt & pepper and the crushed chilli flakes (optional) now mash the contents with a potato masher to release juices and mix well and set to the side.

Take a shallow frying pan and add the oil, place over a medium heat and once the oil has heated add the sliced mushrooms and cook for 3-4 minutes turning occasionally (we like to add additional garlic granules at this point) once cooked remove from the heat.

Place the sourdough pizza base onto the pizza tray. Generously spoon the chunky tomato sauce and cover the base, Scatter the spinach leaves over the top, Now take the rest of the toppings, yellow pepper, red onion, the mushrooms you just cooked &

jalapenos and spread them evenly across the pizza. Finish by crumbling some of the feta over the top and leave a few of the cubes whole.

Place on the middle shelf in the oven and cook for 10-12 minutes.

Serve with any salad or side of your choice and enjoy.

USEFUL TIP

Don't worry if you have any surplus left from the chunky tomato sauce, it goes well in wraps, baguette's and can be used in curry sauces etc.

Chunky Tomato Supreme Pizza

Courgette & Chickpea Shakshuka

This dish is full of flavour, a quick alternative to a traditional bell pepper Shakshuka that can be enjoyed any time of the day.

EQUIPMENT

- Large pot
- Small bowl

INGREDIENTS

Serves 2-3

- 4 garlic cloves
- 1 white onion
- 2 courgette
- 1 tin chickpea
- 2 large tomatoes
- 1 tinned chopped tomatoes
- 1 tsp olive oil
- 1/2 cup water

For the spice mix
- 1 tsp sea salt
- 1 tsp black pepper
- 1/2 cumin powder
- 1 tsp sweet paprika
- 1/2 tsp cinnamon
- 1 tsp coconut sugar

Topping
- scrambled tofu (see page 47)

PREPARATION

Peel and mince the garlic.
Peel and roughly chop the onion.
Cut the courgette into chunky cubes.
Cut tomatoes into chunky cubes
Mix your spices in a small bowl.

METHOD

Heat up the oil in the large pot, add the onion and cook until softened. Add the courgette, chickpea, garlic, chopped fresh tomatoes and your spice mix, mix well and simmer for 2-3 minutes stirring frequently.

Add the water and tinned tomatoes, cover with the lid, lower the heat slightly and simmer for 10-15 minutes.

Serve hot and top with our delicious scrambled tofu.

Courgette & Chickpea Shakshuka

Fire on a stick Tofu

This quick and easy way of serving tofu can be a great accompaniment to many different dishes, and we like this one hot.

EQUIPMENT

- Skewers (longer than the oven dish)
- Deep oven dish
- Tofu Press (optional)

INGREDIENTS

Serves 2-3

- 1 block of firm tofu

For the marinade
- 120 ml tomato ketchup of your choice (we use M&S ketchup)
- melinda's red savina pepper sauce (or a hot chilli sauce of your choice) to taste
- 1 tsp garlic granules
- 1 tsp onion granules

PREPARATION

Press the Tofu to drain off any excess water.

METHOD

Cut the tofu into medium sized cubes and set to the side.

Add all the marinade ingredients into a bowl and use a fork to mix well. Once mixed, add the cubed tofu and gently coat in the marinade.

Carefully thread the tofu cubes onto skewers then place the skewers into an oven dish so the ends of the skewers are overlapping the edges of the oven dish so the tofu does not touch the bottom. Place under a grill and cook for 10-15 minutes, rotating the skewers every few minutes to ensure the tofu cooks evenly. Once cooked, serve and enjoy.

USEFUL TIP
Try experimenting with this fiery tofu and serve in kebabs, in wraps, on pizzas, on jacket potatoes and in stir frys etc

Fire on a Stick Tofu

Funky Funghi Pizza

USEFUL TIP
Don't worry if you have any surplus left from the garlic mushrooms or chunky tomato sauce, they both go well in wraps, additions to curries, baguette's etc

We are both great lovers of mushrooms & garlic so putting our twist on this traditional funghi pizza came easily.

EQUIPMENT

- Pizza tray
- Grater or blender
- Medium pan

INGREDIENTS

Serves 2-3

- sourdough pizza base (we use M&S) or you can make your own or choose one of your choice.

For the chunky tomato base sauce
- 5 large sized vine tomatoes (diced)
- 1 x tin of Italian plum tomatoes
- 1.5 tsp of onion granules
- 2 tsp of garlic granules
- 1 tbsp of Italian seasoning
- 1 heaped tsp of smoked paprika
- pinch of sea salt & pepper to taste
- 2 tsp of crushed chilli flakes (optional)

Toppings
- handful of wild rocket
- fresh garlic cloves
- vegan feta (we use M&S plant kitchen)

PREPARATION

Take the mushrooms and either grate or blend (using the grating blade). Cut the vine tomatoes into chunky cubes.
Peel and slice the fresh garlic.

METHOD

Preheat the oven to 220°C/425°F/gas 7.

Place a medium pan over a moderate heat and add the 2 tablespoons of vegan butter, once this has melted add the grated mushrooms, garlic granules and dried parsley, stir in well and cook for 4 minutes, add the soy sauce and season with sea salt. Cook for 15 minutes or until the mushrooms get slightly crispy. Set to the side.

In a large bowl add the cubed vine tomatoes, tin of Italian plum tomatoes, onion granules, garlic granules, Italian seasoning, smoked paprika, salt & pepper and the crushed chilli flakes (optional) give it all a good mix then mash the contents with a potato masher to break it up a little and release the juices, mix well.

Place the sourdough pizza base onto the pizza tray. Generously spoon the chunky tomato sauce and cover the base, take the wild rocket & scatter over the sauce, then put heaped spoonfuls of the garlic mushrooms over the top.

Finish by adding some feta cubes & sliced garlic then pop it into the middle shelf of the oven and cook for 10-12 minutes.

Serve with any sides of your choice and enjoy.

Funky Funghi Pizza

Green Risotto with Mushrooms and Roasted Tomatoes

This is a 'green' variation of one of our most favourite dishes: a traditional mushroom risotto. Our rich green pesto completely transforms it into a truly exquisite, restaurant grade quality dish.

EQUIPMENT

- Food Processor or Blender
- Grater
- Baking tray

INGREDIENTS

Serves 4-5

For the pesto
- 4 tbsp cashew nuts
- a big bunch of coriander
- a bunch of mint
- 1 clove garlic
- 3 tbsp nutritional yeast
- 1/2 tsp sea salt
- 1/2 tsp black pepper
- 2 tbsp olive oil
- 1 lemon
- 2 tbsp water to loosen

For the roast tomatoes
- 2 cups cherry tomatoes
- splash olive oil
- pinch of sea salt

For the risotto
- 300g arborio rice
- 2 tbsp olive oil
- 2 onions
- 1 cup of frozen green pea
- 1 broccoli
- 4 garlic cloves
- 1/3 cup white wine vinegar
- 5 cups veg stock
- 1 cup mushrooms of your choice
- 2 large handfuls of baby leaf spinach
- 5 tbsp nutritional yeast
- zest 1 lemon + juice
- 1 tsp chilli flakes
- 1 tsp sea salt
- lots of black pepper
- 1 cup green pesto
- 2 tbsp olive oil
- pinch salt
- vegan butter

PREPARATION

For the pesto
Roughly chop the coriander.
Remove mint leaves from the stalks.
Peel and mince the garlic.
Juice the lemon.

For the risotto
Roughly chopped the onion.
Peel and mince the garlic.
Cut the broccoli into florets.
Cut mushrooms into chunky cubes.
Juice the lemon and zest

For the tomatoes
Place the tomatoes on the baking tray,
sprinkle with sea salt and drizzle with
olive oil.

Peel and slice the fresh garlic.

METHOD

Add all the pesto ingredients to your
food processor or blender and blitz until
everything is combined to the texture
you like. You may need to scrape the
sides down a few times, once done set
to the side.

Preheat the oven to 220°C/425°F/gas 7

Heat up the oil in a large pan on
medium heat then add in the chopped
onions. Cook for 5 minutes until
softened and browned. Add the garlic
and mix with onion, then add broccoli
florets and green peas, stir to combine
and cook for a further 5 minutes.

Add the rice, chopped mushrooms and
the white wine vinegar to the pan and
stir thoroughly to combine.
Pour 4 cups of vegetable stock,
decrease the heat to low and cook for
around 25 minutes until all the liquid
is absorbed. Reserve 1 cup of stock
and add more if needed. Stir every
few minutes to prevent the rice from
sticking.

At this point place the tomatoes in the
preheated oven on the middle shelf and
roast for around 20 minutes.

Once the rice is soft and all liquid has
evaporated, stir in 1 cup of pesto along
with the spinach leaves and add in half
of the zest and juice of your lemon, salt,
pepper, chilli flakes and nutritional yeast
and stir to combine.

You can serve at this stage or if
you want a super gooey, soft and
comforting Risotto turn off the heat
and pop the lid on and let it sit for 10 -15
minutes.

Top with roast tomatoes, more pesto,
a dollop of vegan butter, and the
remainder of the lemon zest.

Mushroom Risotto

This classic comforting dish is one of our favourites. So simple, but yet it never fails to satisfy. Garnishing with lemon zest just leaves you wanting to go back for more.

EQUIPMENT

- Large pot

INGREDIENTS

Serves 4-5

- 570g Field Mushroom
- 1 Large White Onion
- 4 Garlic Cloves
- 1 tbsp Olive Oil
- 900ml of vegetable stock
- 1 tsp Sea Salt
- 1 heaped tsp Cracked Black Pepper
- 1/2 bunch of Coriander
- 1 tbsp Italian Seasoning
- 1/2 cup of Apple Cider vinegar
- 4 tbsp of Nutritional Yeast
- 350g of Risotto Rice
- Vegan Butter
- Lemon Zest

PREPARATION

Chop the field mushrooms into cubes.
Chop the white onion into small cubes.
Peel and chop the garlic.
Remove stems and roughly chop the coriander.

METHOD

Place a large pot over a medium heat and add the olive oil, once hot add the chopped onion & garlic and cook until the onion softens. Once done add the mushrooms to the pot and give a good stir to mix together, cook for 5 minutes and stir occasionally.

Next add the risotto rice and mix in well, keep stirring and cook for 2 minutes. Next add half of the stock and the apple cider vinegar and cook for a further 10 minutes, stirring occasionally.

Add the remainder of the stock along with the seasoning and cook on a low heat for another 15 minutes or until the rice is soft and most of the liquid has been absorbed, stir frequently to prevent the rice sticking to the pot.

Remove from the heat and add the nutritional yeast and chopped coriander and mix in well. Serve immediately with a good dollop of vegan butter and finish with grating some lemon zest over the top.

Serve with some garlic bread or salad of your choice.

Mushroom Risotto

Pastry Tart

We are constantly on the go and wanted to create something for lunch times which was both tasty and yet easy to throw together and this pastry tart was the perfect choice.

EQUIPMENT

- Baking Tray
- Blender

INGREDIENTS

Serves 2-3

- Base - Puff pastry

Pesto
- 1 large bunch coriander
- 1 small bunch mint
- 1 tin green pea (250g net/ drained weight)
- 2 limes juiced
- 3 tbsp sunflower seeds
- 2 tbsp nutritional yeast
- 1 tsp black pepper
- 1tsp garlic granules
- 3 tbsp extra virgin olive oil
- salt to taste
- 4-5 tbsp water to thin it out

Toppings
- a few plum tomatoes
- yellow pepper
- portobello mushroom
- red onion
- fresh garlic
- vegan feta

PREPARATION

Remove the stems from the coriander & mint.
Halve the plum tomatoes.
Deseed and slice the yellow pepper.
Peel and thinly slice the red onion.
Peel and thinly slice the fresh garlic.
Slice the portobello mushrooms.
Juice the limes.

METHOD

Preheat the oven to 220°C/425°F/gas 7

For the Pesto, place the coriander,mint,green peas,lime juice,sunflower seeds,nutritional yeast,black pepper,garlic granules,olive oil and salt to taste into the blender and pulse until you reach your desired texture, if the mix is too thick you can add a little water to thin it out, once done set to the side.

Take the puff pastry and roll it out and place on baking paper then on the baking tray, turn the edges in on themselves to create a rim. Now take the pesto mix and spoon a few generous heaped spoonfuls and spread evenly across the base of the pastry. You can now start to decorate the top

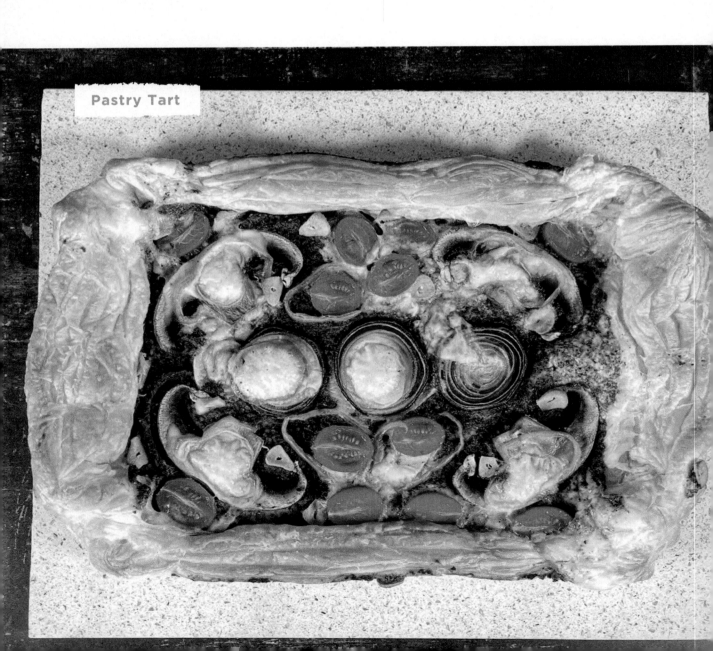

Pastry Tart

Crispy Shawarma Oyster Mushroom Kebab

A healthier alternative to the classic kebab. This dish is packed with some awesome flavours and a must try as it is simply divine.

EQUIPMENT

- Pestle & Mortar
- Grater
- Food Processor or Blender
- Medium sized pan
- Small mixing bowl

INGREDIENTS

Serves 4-6

Mushrooms
- 650g oyster mushrooms
- 2 tbsp olive oil
- 2 tbsp soy sauce
- 6 focaccia flatbreads

Shawarma Spices
- 1 tsp smoked paprika
- 1 tsp caraway seeds (toasted)
- 1 tsp cumin seeds (toasted)
- 1 tsp sage
- 1 tsp oregano
- 1 tsp onion granules
- 1 tsp dried mint

Kebab Fillers
- Hot Aromatic Green Sauce (see page 196)
- fire on a stick tofu marinade (see page 112)
- turkish style salad (see page 134)
- red cabbage & apple salad (see page 66)
- roasted red pepper hummus (see page 200)

PREPARATION

Lightly toast the caraway seeds & the cumin seeds, then grind them in a pestle and mortar and reduce to a coarse powder.
Tear the oyster mushrooms into chunky strips.

METHOD

Add the caraway & cumin powder you prepared into a bowl along with the rest of the shawarma spice ingredients, using a fork mix until they have all blended together.

Place the frying pan over a medium/ high heat and add the olive oil, when the oil has heated add the pre torn oyster mushrooms and cook for roughly 2 to 3 minutes shaking occasionally to turn the mushrooms. Add the soy sauce and cook for a further 2-3 minutes, now take a generous pinch of the shawarma spice mix and sprinkle over the mushrooms and give them a stir and let them cook 2 to 3 minutes.

Add another generous pinch of the shawarma mix and once again give them a good stir, at this point keep stirring every 20/30 seconds to ensure the mushrooms are evenly coated. Cook for another 2 minutes or until they have reached the desired crispiness and set to the side.

Place a clean pan over a medium heat and gently heat the focaccia bread for 1 minute, ensuring you turn the bread every 20 seconds to heat evenly (you only want to warm the bread).

Once cooked you are ready to serve with the rest of the suggested kebab fillers (see page numbers). Ensure you take the cook/prep times into account so you can serve this feast all together at the same time. Enjoy.

Chrispy Shawarma Oyster Mushroom Kebab

Spag Bowl

We absolutely love a good old spag bowl "who doesn't", here we put our own spin on this classic favourite of many, and turn it into a simply scrumptious comforting dish guaranteed to impress you and your guests.

EQUIPMENT

- Potato Masher
- Grater
- Large Pot
- Deep pan
- Large airtight container
- Large mixing bowl

INGREDIENTS

Serves 4-6

- 500g durum wheat spaghetti
- 315g field mushrooms
- 320g chestnut mushrooms
- 2 carrot
- 1 stick of celery
- 1 red onion
- 1 tin green lentils in water (drained)
- 2 yellow pepper
- fresh basil
- lemon zest
- 2 tbsp olive oil

Marinade
- 2 tbsp soy sauce
- 1 tsp garlic granules
- 1 tsp onion granules
- cracked black pepper to taste
- sea salt to taste

Chunky Tomato Sauce
- 650g large vine tomatoes
- 1 tin plum tomatoes
- 1 vegetable stock cube
- 1 tbsp nutritional yeast
- sea salt to taste
- cracked black pepper to taste
- 1 tsp garlic granules
- 1 tsp onion granules
- 1 tbsp italian seasoning
- 1 tsp chilli flakes
- 1 tsp dark soy

PREPARATION

Chop the field & chestnut mushrooms into small cubes.
Peel & chop the carrots, red onion & yellow pepper into small cubes.
Roughly chop the vine tomatoes.
Break down the vegetable stock cube in a quarter cup of boiling water.

METHOD

Add the field & chestnut mushrooms into a large airtight container and add the Marinade ingredients, put the lid on and give the container a good shake to coat the mushrooms with the marinade, set to the side (you can do this in advance if you like, the longer they are marinating the better they will taste).

Place the chopped vine tomatoes into a large mixing bowl, add the tin of plum tomatoes, vegetable stock, Nutritional Yeast, garlic & onion granules, italian seasoning, salt & pepper, dark soy & chilli flakes then mix well with a spoon, take the potato masher and mash the ingredients so the tomatoes break up & release some juice, then set to the side.

Place a deep frying pan over a medium/high heat and add the olive oil, wait for the oil to heat up then add the chopped onion and chopped carrot, cook for 3-5 minutes stirring occasionally until they have softened, now add the marinated mushrooms and cook for a further 5-8 minutes stirring occasionally. Add the chunky tomato sauce and mix in well, reduce the flame to low and add the yellow pepper, stir in and simmer for 30 minutes, stirring every 5 minutes.

Bring a deep pan of water to the boil and add a good pinch of salt, add the spaghetti pasta and boil for 2 minutes then reduce the heat and simmer for a further 8 minutes stirring occasionally to check the firmness of the pasta, you are aiming for al dente. Once the spaghetti is ready, remove from the heat and pour into a colander, rinse with boiling water.

Plate up the spaghetti and add 2 generous spoonfuls of the sauce.

Garnish with fresh Basil & grated Lemon zest. Enjoy.

USEFUL TIP
This amazing sauce can be used with so many other things, you can add it to - jacket potatoes, wraps, pizza etc

Spag Bowl

Spiralized Zucchini with Spicy Ragu

Sometimes we like a change from pasta and spiralized zucchini is the perfect replacement and it also brings a vibrant colour to the plate.

EQUIPMENT

- Spiralizer
- Potato masher
- Deep pan
- Grater
- Large mixing bowl

INGREDIENTS

Serves 4-6

- 2 x zucchini (yellow or green)

For the Ragu
- 8 x vine tomatoes & sweet plum tomatoes
- 1 x tbsp italian seasoning
- 1 x level tsp cracked black pepper
- sea salt - to taste
- 1 x level tsp onion granules
- 1 x level tsp garlic granules
- 1 x level tsp chilli flakes (optional)
- 1 x red sweet pepper
- 1 x orange sweet pepper
- 5 x field mushrooms
- 1 x red onion
- 1 x tbsp dark soy sauce
- 1 x tbsp olive oil

Dressings
- fresh basil
- vegan feta (crumbled)
- lemon zest

PREPARATION

Dice both the vine & plum tomatoes.
Deseed and roughly chop the sweet peppers.
Finely chop the mushrooms.
Peel & finely chop the onion.
Spiralize the zucchini.

METHOD

Put the diced tomatoes,Italian seasoning,cracked black pepper,sea salt,garlic granules,onion granules & chilli flakes into a large bowl and mix thoroughly, then use a potato masher to gently squash and release the juices then put to one side.

Next in a deep frying pan pour 1 tablespoon of olive oil and place over a medium heat, add the finely chopped red onion and cook until translucent & soft, then add the finely chopped mushrooms and cook for 3 to 4 minutes, then add the dark soy sauce and cook for a further 4 minutes.

Now take the bowl of spicy ragu you put to the side and add it to the pan and stir in gently. Add the roughly chopped red and orange sweet pepper and stir in, reduce the heat to a low and allow to cook for 20 minutes, stirring occasionally, taste and season with salt and pepper as necessary.

Take the spiralized zucchini and dress on the plate, then top with the spicy ragu and finish off by crumbling the vegan feta over the dish and sprinkle some torn fresh basil topped with some freshly grated lemon zest.

USEFUL TIP

If you end up with too much of the spicy ragu, don't throw it away as it can be used in many ways - add to curry sauces, use as pizza base sauce, in salads, wraps etc.

Spiralized Zucchini with Spicy Ragu

Traditional Shakshuka

This dish originates from Israel but its variations are served all over Northern Africa. If you are a lover of peppers this stunning dish is a must try.

EQUIPMENT

- Large Pot

INGREDIENTS

Serves 3-4

- 1 white onion
- 5 large garlic cloves
- 2 red bell peppers
- 1 yellow bell pepper
- 1 fresh hot chilli
- 6 tomatoes on the vine
- 2 large handfuls baby leaf spinach
- 1 tsp olive oil
- 1 tsp cumin seeds
- 1 tsp caraway seeds
- 1 heaped tsp smoked paprika
- 1 tsp coconut sugar
- a small pinch saffron
- sea salt to taste
- 1 tsp cracked black pepper
- 150ml water

PREPARATION

Chop the onion into chunky cubes. Chop the bell pepper into chunky cubes.

Peel and chop the garlic.
Roughly chop the tomatoes.
Deseed and finely chop the chilli.

METHOD

Add the oil to the pot and place over a medium heat. Once heated add the cumin and caraway seeds and cook for 1 minute or until you can smell the aromas rising.

Add the onion and garlic and cook until translucent. Then add the peppers, chillies, and tomatoes with the rest of the spices. Reduce the heat to a low and cook for around 10 minutes with the lid on, adding 150ml water half way through. Once the peppers get soft it's time to add 2-3 handfuls of spinach leaves and stir in.

Remove from the heat and allow it to stand for two minutes before serving.

Best served with tofu scramble (see page 47) and chopped coriander.

Traditional Shakshuka

Turkish Style Salad

This has to be one of the easiest salads to prepare and yet it can be served with a large variety of dishes or simply enjoyed on its own.

EQUIPMENT

- Large Salad bowl
- Grater

INGREDIENTS

Serves 3-4

- 1/2 cucumber
- 1 bunch parsley
- 1 bunch chive
- 1 red onion
- 1 pomegranate
- 275g sweet plum tomatoes
- 70g pistachio kernels
- 1 lemon

PREPARATION

Thinly chop the parsley & chives.
Chop the cucumber into small cubes.
Peel and roughly chop the onion.
Quarter the plum tomatoes.
Chop the pistachios.
Grate the lemon.
Juice the lemon.

METHOD

Add all of the prepared ingredients into the large salad bowl and give a good mix.

Next cut the pomegranate in half, Hold it in your hand face down over the salad bowl and start beating the top with a wooden spoon or spatula in order to release the seeds easily.

Add the lemon zest and juice to the salad, season with the sea salt and black pepper to taste, then mix well and serve on its own or as an accompaniment to anything of your choice.

Turkish Style Salad

Tuscan Butter Bean Soup

An Italian classic that can simply be enjoyed all year round.

EQUIPMENT

- Large pot

INGREDIENTS

Serves 3-4

- 1 shallot peeled and diced
- 1/2 leek chopped
- 1 tablespoons of olive oil teaspoon
- 1/2 of salt
- 3 cloves garlic peeled and chopped finely
- 1 celery stalks halved and chopped
- 1 carrot quartered, peeled and chopped
- 0.5 courgette quartered and chopped
- 3 diced tomatoes
- 120g spinach
- 400 g tin butter beans drained
- cup 1/2 of fresh basil chopped
- 800ml vegetable stock

PREPARATION

Peel and dice the shallot.
Chop the leek.
Peel and finely chop the garlic.
Half and chop the celery.
Peel, quarter & chop the carrot.
Quarter & chop the courgette.
Dice the tomatoes.
Chop the fresh basil.

METHOD

Heat the olive oil in a large pot over a medium to low heat and add the leek, shallots, garlic, celery, salt, carrots and courgette and cook slowly for 15 to 20 minutes so that the vegetables sweat out their flavours, but be careful not to brown.

Add the tinned tomatoes and stir into the vegetables and cook for a few minutes. Add the beans, half the basil and stir through the mixture (I like to squash some of the beans into the mix at this point to release their flavour and help thicken the soup) and cook for 10 minutes.

Add the vegetable stock and bring the soup to a boil before lowering the heat to simmer for a further 25 to 30 minutes. Just before serving add the spinach leaves and remaining basil and give a quick stir to mix in.

Serve with your favourite crusty bread & butter.

Tuscan Butter Bean Soup

Mexican

Baked avocados

Baked avocados can be enjoyed with various toppings, so feel free to experiment with different sauces and fillings that you may have left as a surplus in the fridge. Here's our take featuring our Mexican Buckwheat married with an umami flavour of Kimchi.

EQUIPMENT

- Baking tray
- Sharp knife

INGREDIENTS

Serves 2-4

- 2 avocados
- mexican buckwheat (see page 152)
- kimchi (see page 168)
- vegan feta cubes

METHOD

Preheat the oven to 200°C/400°F/gas 6

Cut the avocados in half lengthwise and remove the stone. Hold the avocado in your hand (skin side in your palm) and make a criss-cross pattern using a sharp knife while being careful not to go too deep and cut yourself.
Place the avocado halves on the baking tray and top with the buckwheat and vegan feta cubes or vegan cheese of your choice.
Place the baking tray on the middle shelf and bake for 15 minutes. Remove from the oven and top up with Kimchi.

Serve hot with Cashew Sour Cream (see page 192) or Mango Chilli Ketchup (see page 198)

Baked Avocados

Burritos

This scrumptious meal simply uses our flagship Mexican dishes and can be enjoyed any time of the day. Feel free to experiment and use one of our hummus instead of guacamole, or rice instead of buckwheat. A unique experience every time!

EQUIPMENT

- Baking tray

INGREDIENTS

Serves 2-4

- 4 tortilla wraps
- Crunchy Guacamole (see page 148)
- Mexican Buckwheat (see page 152)
- Chilli Non-Carne (see page 145)
- Mango Salsa (see page 150)
- Cashew Sour Cream (see page 192)
- Vegan cheese of your choice

METHOD

Preheat the oven to 200°C/400°F/gas 6

Spread guacamole on the entire surface of the tortilla wraps. Place the Mexican Buckwheat in the middle, top up with Chilli Non-Carne and sprinkle with vegan cheese. Wrap and place on the baking tray.

Place the baking tray on the middle shelf in the oven and bake for 5 minutes to warm it up.

Serve with Mango Salsa and Cashew Sour Cream.

Burritos

Cheesy Blue Nachos

A wonderful starter to serve at the parties or simply enjoy with your partner, family and friends during Netflix evenings.

EQUIPMENT

- Oven dish
- Blender
- Small pot
- Spatula

INGREDIENTS

Serves 4-6

- 150g blue corn tortilla chips (we got ours from M&S)
- jalapenos

Cheesy sauce
- 150g cashews
- 300ml water
- 1 lemon

Seasoning Mix
- 1 tbsp garlic granules
- 1 tbsp onion granules
- 1/2 tsp turmeric
- 2 tbsp nutritional yeast
- 1tsp sea salt
- 1/2 tsp black pepper
- 1 tsp tapioca flour

PREPARATION

Soak the cashews in boiled and slightly cooled water for 1 hour then strain and set to the side.

Juice the lemon.

Mix all the seasoning including tapioca flour in a small bowl and set aside.

METHOD

Preheat the oven to 200°C/400°F/gas 6

Lay the blue corn tortilla chips in the ovenproof dish, so that they fully cover the bottom.

Blend the cashews, water, lemon juice and the seasoning until you reach a perfectly smooth consistency. Tip into a small pot and use the spatula to scrape the sides.

Place the pot on low heat and cook for 10 minutes stirring continuously to prevent the cheesy sauce from sticking to the bottom and burning. After around 10 minutes, you will reach a stretchy texture, which means your sauce is ready. Remove from the heat and pour on top of the tortilla. Place a few jalapenos on top.

Place the nachos in the oven on the middle shelf and bake until the edges of the cheesy sauce start going brown for around 15 minutes. Remove the dish from the oven.

Serve whilst still hot topped with our Chunky Guacamole (see page 148) and Mango Salsa (see page 150)

Cheesy Blue Nachos

Chilli Non-Carne

This fingerlicking flagship Mexican dish is full of deep flavour with a rich cacao aftertaste that will leave you in awe and simply wanting more.

EQUIPMENT

- Medium pan
- Large pan
- Mixing Bowl

INGREDIENTS

Serves 6-8

- 300g mushrooms
- 1 red onion
- 4 cloves garlic
- 2 fresh red chillies
- 2 celery sticks
- 1 carrot
- 2 sweet red peppers
- 1/2 bunch coriander
- 2 tomatoes
- 1 tbsp olive oil
- 1/2 tsp salt
- 1/2 tsp black pepper
- 2 tbsp tomato puree
- 200ml red wine
- 2tbsp soy sauce
- 1 tbsp red wine vinegar
- 1 tinned tomato
- 1 tin cannellini beans
- 1 tin red kidney beans
- 4 tsp maple syrup
- 1 tbsp raw cacao powder

Spice Mix

- 1 tsp chilli powder
- 1 tsp ground cumin
- 1 tbsp smoked paprika
- 1 tsp sweet paprika
- 1 tsp cinnamon
- 3 bay leaves
- 1/2 tsp oregano
- 1/2 tsp marjoram
- 1/2 tsp thyme

PREPARATION

Mix all your spices in a bowl and set them aside.
Finely chop the mushrooms.
Peel and finely chop the red onion.
Peel and mince the garlic.
Deseed and finely chop the red chillies.
Cut the celery sticks lengthwise into 3-4 long strips and then finely chop.
Peel and cut the carrot into small cubes
Deseed and chop the red pepper.
Roughly chop the coriander including stalks.
Roughly cube the tomatoes.
Drain and rinse the beans.

METHOD

Heat the oil in the medium pan on medium heat. Once the oil is hot, add the mushrooms with a pinch of sea salt and black pepper and cook for 10 minutes until browned. Remove from the heat and set aside.

Next, heat up a little oil in the large pan over medium heat, add the onion, garlic and celery and cook for around 5 minutes until soft. At this stage, add the red pepper, chilli, carrot, half of the coriander including stalks and spice mix and stir well so that all vegetables are covered in the spices. Decrease the heat to low and simmer for 5 minutes.

Pour the red wine, soy sauce, and red wine vinegar in and increase the heat to high, stirring continuously until the liquid is reduced by half and the alcohol aroma evaporates.

Add the tinned chopped tomatoes, cubed fresh tomatoes, tomato puree and maple syrup and combine well with the other ingredients. Decrease the heat to medium and simmer for a further 5-7 minutes.

Add the cooked mushrooms along with raw cacao powder and beans, reduce the heat even further to let it simmer gently, stirring occasionally for 15 minutes or until it reaches your desired texture. You can simmer it for longer for a richer flavour slowly adding more water to prevent the ingredients from sticking to the bottom of the pan and keeping the right consistency.

Take off the heat and stir in the coriander leaves. Serve hot with our Cashew Sour Cream (see page 192) and Mexican Buckwheat (see page 152)

USEFUL TIP
This scrumptious dish keeps well in the freezer for up to 6 months.

It can also be enjoyed cold in sandwiches and wraps.

Crunchy Guacamole

Now there is guacamole, and then there is our guacamole! It is a must-try for all avocado lovers out there.

EQUIPMENT

- Sharp knife

INGREDIENTS

Serves 3-4

- 2 ripe avocados
- 1 red onion
- 1/2 tsp sea salt
- 1/2 tsp black pepper
- 1 red chilli
- 1 tbsp nutritional yeast

METHOD

Cut the avocado lengthwise in half and remove the stone, spoon out the avocado and Place in a bowl, mash with a fork until you get a smooth texture then set to the side.

Peel and finely chop the red onion and add to the smashed avocado. Add all the spices and mix everything until well combined.

Serve with your favourite Mexican dishes or on top of toasted sourdough bread and enjoy.

USEFUL TIP

Crunchy guacamole will stay fresh in an airtight container for up to 2 days.

Crunchy Guacamole

Mango Salsa

A truly delicious version of salsa with a hint of chilli and a sweet aftertaste of mango and a delicate flavour note of lime and tomatoes. It's so delicious that you will want the whole bowl for yourself.

EQUIPMENT

- Serving bowl

INGREDIENTS

Serves 3-4

- 400g cherry tomatoes
- 1 soft mango
- 1 bunch coriander
- 1 red chilli
- 2 limes
- 1/2 tsp sea salt
- 1 tsp black pepper

METHOD

Roughly chop the coriander and place it in the bowl, deseed the chilli and chop thinly.

Peel the mango and cut into small cubes, then halve the cherry tomatoes.

Place all the ingredients in the bowl, squeeze the two limes, add the salt and black pepper and mix well.

Serve as a side to your Mexican dishes.

USEFUL TIP

We often use any surplus we may have left in wraps and burgers.

Mango Salsa

Mexican Buckwheat

It is usually rice that is served with the Mexican dishes, but we feel that buckwheat, this incredibly healthy and nutritious grain, doesn't get used too much in most cuisines. That's how the idea of using buckwheat as a part of our Mexican Feast was born.

EQUIPMENT

- Large pot

INGREDIENTS

Serves 4

- 200g buckwheat
- 1 lime
- 1 hot red chilli
- 1 tbsp butter
- 1 tsp sea salt

PREPARATION

Squeeze the lime.
Deseed and finely chop the chilli.

METHOD

Cook the buckwheat as per the instructions on the packaging.
Once ready, add the sea salt, lime juice, butter and chopped chilli and mix well.

Serve instead of rice with our Mexican dishes or any meals of your choice.

USEFUL TIP

Buckwheat can be also enjoyed cold mixed with salads, which will create a more filling alternative during colder months.

Spicy Cauliflower Bites

Smooth cauliflower covered in crunchy breadcrumbs and with a rich flavour of BBQ & Sriracha coating that can be served as a starter or an accompaniment to the main meal.

USEFUL TIP

These cauliflower bites are exceptional as a pizza topping, in wraps and salads.

EQUIPMENT

- Baking tray
- 2 bowls
- Small pot

INGREDIENTS

Serves 2-3

- 1/2 cauliflower

For the batter
- 120g plain flour
- 240ml plant-based milk
- 2 tsp garlic granules
- 2 tsp onion granules
- 1 tsp sweet paprika
- 1/2 tsp sea salt
- 1/2 tsp black pepper
- 1/2 tsp nutmeg
- 150g breadcrumbs

For the coating sauce
- 90g dairy-free butter
- 100g BBQ sauce
- 50g sriracha

PREPARATION

Cut the cauliflower into small florets
Finely chop the mushrooms.

METHOD

Preheat the oven to 200°C/400°F/gas 6

Firstly, prepare the batter. Mix plant-based milk, flour, garlic granules, onion granules, sweet paprika, sea salt, black pepper and nutmeg in a bowl and whisk into a lump-free, smooth batter. Put the breadcrumbs into the second bowl.

Place the cauliflower florets into the batter and make sure they are evenly coated. Take them one by one and dip them in the bread crumbs, roll them around to give them a good coat. Repeat this with all the florets.

Line the coated broccoli florets onto the baking tray and place on the middle shelf and cook for 20 minutes. In the meantime, melt the butter in the small pot. Once melted add the BBQ sauce and Sriracha and cook for 3 minutes, whisking continuously to combine all the ingredients well.

Take the cauliflower out of the oven after 20 minutes and cover generously in the coating sauce mix. Return to the oven for further 20-25 minutes until the coating gets crispy and the cauliflower has softened.

Serve the cauliflower wings hot with our Cashew Sour Cream as a dip (see page 192).

Spicy Cauliflower Bites

Oriental

Buddha Bowl

Buddha Bowl is the perfect comfort meal for us. It originates from the idea of a balanced meal. Balance is key in Buddhism. The story says that Buddha carried his food bowl to fill it with whatever bits of vegetarian food villagers would offer him. It may also refer to a big, round Buddha belly shape. Buddha bowls are always full and filled with rice or whole grains, roasted veggies, a dressing and protein (usually tofu, tempeh, beans or lentils) and is a perfectly balanced meal.

EQUIPMENT

- Griddle pan
- Wok or deep pan
- Spiralizer
- Pot

INGREDIENTS

Serves 3-4

- 180g quinoa
- oriental red cabbage (see page 162)
- kimchi (see page 168)
- 1/2 cucumber
- 1 carrot
- saffron hummus (see page 202)
- 2 tbsp sesame seeds
- 2 tbsp walnuts
- 2 tbsp pistachios
- sea salt, to taste
- black pepper, to taste
- crushed chilli to taste
- toasted sesame oil, to drizzle

For sweet potato
- 1 sweet potato
- 1 tbsp olive oil
- 1/2 tsp sea salt
- 1 tbsp nutritional yeast

For tamari pak choi and edamame
- 2 pak choi
- 160g edamame
- 3 garlic cloves
- 2tbsp cranberries
- 3tbsp tamari sauce
- 1tbsp rice vinegar
- 1tsp olive oil

For crispy tempeh
- tempeh
- 1 tsp chilli flakes (optional)
- 2 tbsp tamari sauce
- sea salt, to taste
- cracked black pepper, to taste

- 1 tbsp olive oil

PREPARATION

Peel and slice the sweet potato into thick slices and then cube. Transfer into a bowl, add salt and nutritional yeast. Mix to cover the sweet potato evenly and set aside for 10 minutes.

Roughly chop the pak choi, mince the

garlic and cook the edamame if using from frozen (no need to cook if it is fresh).
Place dried cranberries in a bowl and cover with hot water.
Spiralise the carrot and cut the cucumber into strips. Set aside.
Roughly chop walnuts and pistachios. Set aside.

METHOD

Preheat the oven to 220°C/425°F/gas 7

When the oven reaches the right temperature, transfer sweet potato cubes from the bowl onto the baking tray and spread them evenly. Bake on the middle shelf for 30 mins. Check halfway through and turn them.

Cook quinoa following the instructions on the packet (usually around 15 minutes).

When the sweet potato starts getting soft and crispy, prepare the tempeh. Slice it in 1cm slices and place it on a preheated griddle pan with a bit of oil on it. Fry both sides, turning every 2 minutes. When the tempeh starts getting light brown and crispy, drizzle with tamari sauce and add crushed chilli flakes, salt and pepper. Turn to the other side and repeat. When the outside of the tempeh gets brown and crispy, turn off the heat and set to the side.

Check the sweet potatoes at this stage, and if they are getting brown and crispy on the outside, turn off the oven,

so they don't get burned.

Add 1 teaspoon of olive oil into a wok or deep pan and when the oil is hot add the garlic. Cook for 1-minute stirring occasionally to prevent it from burning. Strain the cranberries and add to the garlic along with edamame beans. Stir continuously for 2-3 minutes and then add the pak choi, tamari sauce and rice vinegar. Cook for another couple of minutes until the pak choi leaves are wilted, remove from the heat.

Now it's time to assemble your Buddha bowl. Start with spiralized carrots and cucumber by placing them in a bowl next to each other. Then add Oriental Red Cabbage, quinoa, kimchi, pak choi with edamame, sweet potatoes and tempeh. Add a generous spoonful of hummus in the middle of the bowl, drizzle with toasted sesame oil, sprinkle with sesame seeds and chopped pistachios and walnuts. Enjoy.

USEFUL TIP

Buddha Bowls are incredibly versatile and can be prepared in many different ways. Feel free to swap the ingredients and experiment with different vegetables, nuts, and seeds or surplus meals that you have in the fridge.

Buddha Bowl

Crispy no Duck Rolls

We absolutely love the combination of ingredients in these delicious rolls, so simple and yet so tasty. We recreated this favourite of ours and along with our homemade hoisin sauce it never fails to please.

EQUIPMENT

- Blender
- Deep Pan/Wok
- Bamboo Steamer Basket

INGREDIENTS

Serves 2-3

- 385g of Oyster Mushrooms

Mushroom Seasoning
- 1 tsp garlic granules
- 1 tbsp chinese 5 spice
- 1 tbsp soy sauce
- 3 large spring onions
- 1/2 cucumber
- 2 tbsp of rapeseed oil
- 12 pancakes for crispy duck (or no duck in our case)

Hoisin Sauce
- 1 cup raisins
- 1 1/4 cups water
- 2 cloves garlic
- 1 tablespoon sesame oil
- 1/2 teaspoon crushed red pepper
- 1 teaspoon wakame flakes
- 1 teaspoon barley miso

PREPARATION

Shred/Tear the oyster mushrooms. Remove the ends and cut the spring onions into strips.
Halve and quarter the cucumber and cut into strips.
Soak the raisins in hot water for up to 20 minutes or until they have softened.
Soak the wakame flakes for 5 minutes
Peel the garlic cloves.

METHOD

Start by making the hoisin sauce, add the raisins and the raisin soaked water into the blender along with soaked wakame flakes and the remaining hoisin sauce ingredients and blend until you get a smooth texture. Once done, transfer the sauce into a serving pot and set to the side.

Add the rapeseed oil to the deep pan/wok and place over a high heat, when the oil is hot add the mushrooms and cook for 3-4 minutes (stirring occasionally). Add the garlic granules and the soy sauce and give a good stir to coat the mushrooms, cook for 2 minutes (stirring occasionally) then add the chinese 5 spice and keep stirring the mushrooms until they develop a nice crispy coat. Set to the side.

Whilst the mushrooms are cooking, place the bamboo steaming basket over a pot of boiling water. Carefully place the pancakes inside and steam for 5-6 minutes (or you can place in a microwave for 20 seconds).

Plate the mushrooms, spring onion & cucumber and serve with the pancakes and hoisin sauce. Roll and enjoy.

USEFUL TIP

The Hoisin sauce can be stored in an airtight container and kept in the fridge for upto 1 week. Try using this sauce in wraps and even just as a dipping sauce.

Crispy no-Duck Rolls

Oriental Red Cabbage with Ginger and Lemongrass

This is originally a Polish dish but we thought we would add to it by giving it a Oriental twist and the outcome was simply delicious.

EQUIPMENT

- Large deep pot
- Mandoline (or sharp knife)

INGREDIENTS

Serves 3-4

- 1 small red cabbage
- 1 tbsp grated ginger
- 3 garlic cloves
- 1 red onion
- 1 fresh lemongrass
- 1 apple
- 1 lemon
- 3 tbsp vegan butter
- 1tsp sea salt
- 1tsp black pepper
- 2tsp coconut sugar
- 1/2 bunch fresh dill

PREPARATION

Slice the red cabbage thinly on the mandolin or with a sharp knife.

Halve and slice the red onion.

Peel and grate approx 2.5in fresh ginger.

Peel and chop the garlic cloves.
Cut the lemongrass in half.
Peel, core and cube an apple.
Chop fresh dill. Juice 1 lemon.

METHOD

Add 1 tablespoon of butter into the large pot and place over a medium heat and let it melt. Add the red onion and cook until soft. Next add the garlic, ginger and red cabbage. Simmer in butter for 2-3 minutes stirring frequently.

Add 1 cup of water along with the lemongrass, apple, sea salt, black pepper and coconut sugar then simmer on medium heat for 20 minutes or until the cabbage is soft. Add more water if needed.

When the cabbage is soft, remove the lemongrass and then add the lemon juice, 2 tablespoons of vegan butter and chopped dill. Mix well to combine.

Serve hot or cold.

USEFUL TIP

It's a great addition to wraps, Buddha bowls, and as a side to many oriental dishes.

Oriental Red Cabbage with Ginger & Lemongrass

Oriental Style Salad

This very simple salad is an excellent accompaniment for many oriental dishes. The unique combination of crunchy kohlrabi paired with aromatic fennel and sweetness of pear will take you on a journey to the Far East.

EQUIPMENT

- Sharp knife
- Salad bowl
- Mandoline (optional)

INGREDIENTS

Serves 3-4

- 1/2 napa cabbage
- 1/2 fresh fennel
- 1/2 kohlrabi
- 1 hot red chilli
- 1 pear
- 100g physalis fruit
- 1 romano pepper

For the dressing
- 4 tbsp tamari sauce
- 4 tsp toasted sesame oil
- 2 tbsp chinese rice vinegar
- 2 tsp maple syrup

METHOD

Thinly slice the napa cabbage, fresh fennel and kohlrabi using a mandoline or sharp knife. Deseed and chop the hot red chilli. Peel and cube the pear. Cut the physalis fruit into halves. Halve the romano pepper, remove the seeds and cut into thin strips. Transfer all the ingredients into the salad bowl.

Mix all the dressing ingredients together and pour over the salad. Mix thoroughly to coat.

Serve and enjoy!

USEFUL TIP

This salad is amazing as a stir fry with added beansprouts and noodles.

Oriental Style Salad

Shiitake Chaga & Miso Broth

Chaga is a medicinal mushroom that has many unique qualities, including strengthening one's immune system. It makes a wonderful strong broth that can be used as a base for many soups, but here we paired it with delicious shiitake mushrooms and miso.

EQUIPMENT

- Large/Medium Pot

INGREDIENTS

Serves 4-5

- 150g shiitake mushrooms
- 2 carrots
- 1 bunch spring onion
- 1 red sweet pepper
- 4 garlic cloves (minced)
- 2 miso sachets
- 2 tbsp nutritional yeast
- 1/2 tsp sea salt
- 1 tsp black pepper
- 1 tbsp dried nettle
- 10 black pitted olives
- 4-5 small size chaga chunks
- 1.5l water

METHOD

Place the chaga chunks in the pot and cover with water, Bring to a boil and simmer on medium heat for 10 mins.

In the meantime, peel and cube the carrots, Slice the sweet red pepper and add to the chaga stock. Halve or quarter the shiitake mushrooms and add them along with the minced garlic, black olives and miso.

Add the sea salt, black pepper and nettle. Simmer for an additional 15 minutes or until the carrots have softened, then add the nutritional yeast and chopped spring onion. Stir in and remove from the heat.

Serve and enjoy.

USEFUL TIP

The soup can be kept in the fridge for 3 days or when frozen will keep for 6 months in the freezer.

Shiitake, Chaga & Miso Broth

Spicy Kimchi

Kimchi is a traditional Korean dish that originated over 3,000 years ago and to this day, Koreans consume it with nearly every meal. It's very satisfying, perhaps because in Korea, the harmony of colour and taste of each meal satisfies the five senses while eating, and each meal is nutritionally balanced.

EQUIPMENT

- Mandoline or sharp knife
- Blender
- Mixing bowl
- Airtight jar or clay crock, like 'Onggi'

INGREDIENTS

Makes 3 litres of kimchi

- 1 white or green cabbage
- 4 tbsp sea salt
- 3 hot chillies (can be decreased to 1 or omitted completely if avoiding heat)
- 40g wakame seaweed
- 4 red onions
- 6 cloves garlic
- 2 - inch ginger
- 1/2 coconut sugar
- 10 medjool dates
- 2 carrots
- 3/4 large daikon
- 3 red sweet peppers
- 2 cups water

PREPARATION

Chop or mandoline the cabbage, place in a large mixing bowl.
Slice 2 red onions.
Slice the carrots.
Cut the daikon in half lengthwise and then slice into half-moons.
Deseed and slice red sweet peppers.
Roughly chop the dates.
Peel and roughly chop the ginger.

METHOD

Sprinkle the shredded cabbage with 4 tablespoons of sea salt and massage well until the cabbage is well softened and starts releasing liquid.
Add sliced sweet pepper, carrots, daikon, 2 sliced onions, wakame seaweed and dates to the cabbage and mix to combine well.

In the blender make a smooth sauce from the remaining ingredients: coconut sugar, ginger, garlic, 2 red onions, chillies and 1 1/2 cup of water. Add and massage into the salty cabbage mix.

Transfer the kimchi into glass jars or clay crock, like 'Onggi', the Korean fermentation pot. Pour an extra inch of water to make sure all ingredients are submerged. Close the jar and keep it in a dark, dry place for 1-3 weeks, but remember to slightly open the jar to release any build up of pressure every few days.

Once ready, move into the fridge where it will last for 6+ months. Enjoy!

USEFUL TIP

This kimchi is a beautiful addition to your wraps, sandwiches, Buddha bowls, lunch boxes, dinners... it's incredibly tasty and versatile, so feel free to experiment.

Spicy Kimchi

Tamari & Tangerine Stir Fry

The key to any good stir fry is preparation. If you take the time to prepare your ingredients before you start to cook, the process becomes extremely simple and in no time at all you have a mouth watering dish sitting in front of you, ready to enjoy.

EQUIPMENT

- Blender
- Wok or Deep Frying pan
- Large pot
- Tongs

INGREDIENTS

Serves 3-4

- 370g oyster mushrooms
- 1 mango
- 300g beansprouts
- 1 carrot
- 1 romano pepper
- 80g baby sweetcorn
- 3 large spring onions
- 100g mangetout
- 1 red chilli
- 250g chilli noodles
- 1 tbsp cold pressed rapeseed oil

For the Mushrooms
- 1 tbsp of soy sauce
- 1 tsp garlic granules
- 2 tsp of chinese 5 spice

Stir Fry Sauce
- 2 tangerines
- 50ml tamari soy sauce

PREPARATION

Halve & quarter the baby sweetcorn.
Halve the mangetout.
Peel & halve the carrots, then slice into thin strips.
Peel & cube the mango.
Roughly chop the red pepper
Remove the ends of the spring onion, then chop in to strips.
Finely chop the red chilli
Blend the tangerines & tamari sauce.

Bring a pot of water to the boil .and add the chilli noodles, boil for 1 minute then remove from the heat and allow to sit for 5 minutes. Drain and put to the side.

METHOD

Add the rapeseed oil to the pan and place over a large heat, once the oil has heated add the oyster mushrooms and cook for 2 minutes turning occasionally. Add the garlic granules & soy sauce and give the mushrooms a good stir to mix in, add the chinese 5 spice and mix again and continue to cook for roughly 3-4 minutes or until the mushrooms have developed a nice crisp coat.

Add the carrots, baby sweetcorn, mangetout, pepper and half of the chillies and stir in. Now add the stir fry sauce and give a good toss to mix together. Add the bean sprouts and half of the spring onion and cook for 2 minutes continuously turning.

Then add the chilli noodles and mix in well, cook for a further 2 minutes. Finally add the mango and gently stir in.

Remove from the heat and serve immediately using the tongs. Finish by garnishing with the remaining spring onion and chillies.

USEFUL TIP

If you have any surplus stir fry left, try using it in wraps for lunch the following day.

Tamari & Tangerine Stir Fry

Traditional British

Creamy Seaside Pie

This simple yet mouthwatering dish has always been the biggest hit with friends and family.

EQUIPMENT

- Medium oven dish
- Large airtight container
- Deep pan
- Large mixing Bowl
- Potato masher

INGREDIENTS

Serves 6

- 2 kg of maris piper potatoes
- 1 leek
- 4 garlic cloves
- 600g mushrooms
- 4 tbsp soya sauce
- 3tbsp olive oil
- 2 nori sheets
- dairy free butter
- 100 white wine vinegar
- 1 tbsp salt
- 50ml soya milk
- 1 tbsp wholegrain mustard
- 2 tbsp nutritional yeast
- 2 tbsp capers
- 1 tbsp capers brine
- 1 lemon
- 10g wakame seaweed
- 175ml soy cream
- 200g frozen pea
- parsley leaves
- black pepper

PREPARATION

Peel and boil the potatoes.
Juice the lemon.

Peel and finely chop the garlic.
Chop the mushrooms into small cubes.
Chop the leek.
Finely chop the nori sheets.

Add the garlic, leek, mushrooms and nori into the airtight container along with the olive oil and marinade for 2 hours.

METHOD

Preheat the oven to 220°C/425°F/gas 7

Place the deep pan over a medium heat and add the olive oil, empty the marinated contents into the pan and cook for around 15 minutes. Add the white wine vinegar and cook for a further 2-3 minutes.

Add the salt, milk, mustard, nutritional yeast, wakame, capers and the capers brine. Add the lemon juice and mix well, let the mushrooms cook until half of the liquid is absorbed.
Add the soy cream and green peas. Remove from the heat and mix in the

parsley. Spoon the contents into the oven dish and spread evenly to cover the base.

Place the boiled potatoes into the large mixing bowl along with the butter and nutritional yeast and mash them until you get a smooth texture, season with salt and pepper.

Spoon the mashed potato on top of the mushroom filling and spread evenly. Run a fork along the surface to create a ridged effect.

Place on the middle shelf of the oven and bake for 25 minutes, then remove from the oven and finish off by placing the oven dish under the grill for 2-3 minutes to add some crisp to the mashed potato.

Serve with our delicious red wine gravy (see page 182) or a gravy of your choice.

Creamy Seaside Pie

Golden Roast Potatoes

Everyone strives for the perfect roast potatoes, we find this method works perfectly for us, delivering the most delicious golden roast spuds time & time again.

EQUIPMENT

- Large Baking tray
- Large deep pot
- Colander

INGREDIENTS

- 8 Maris Piper Potatoes (or the quantity required)
- Olive Oil (a good glug)
- Fresh Rosemary
- 3 Garlic Cloves
- 1 tsp Garlic granules
- 1 tsp Onion granules
- Sea Salt (good pinch)
- Cracked Black Pepper (good pinch)
- 2 tbsp Plain Flour (to sprinkle over the potatoes)

PREPARATION

Peel and wash the potatoes (if you have large potatoes chop them in half)
Peel and crush the garlic cloves.

METHOD

Preheat the oven to 220°C/425°F/gas 7

Place the potatoes in a deep pot of cold water and add a good pinch of salt, then place the pot over a high heat and bring to the boil, allow to boil for 15 minutes or until you feel the potatoes starting to soften (check with a sharp knife or fork) you are looking for the potatoes to be slightly soft. Once ready, remove the potatoes from the pot by pouring them into the colander and allow them to sit for 5 minutes. Take the plain flour and sprinkle it over the potatoes, give the colander a good shake to toss and coat the potatoes in the flour and rough them up a little, allow to sit for another 5 minutes.

Take the large baking tray and coat the bottom with a good glug of olive oil, add the garlic & onion granules, salt & pepper, take a fork and give the oil a good stir to mix in well, now take each potato and give them some individual TLC by gently massage them in the oil so each one is covered, Now add the smashed garlic cloves and throw in a couple sprigs of the rosemary.

Place the baking tray on an upper

shelf in the oven and cook for roughly 1 hour or until the potatoes have developed a lovely golden crisp coat, checking every 20 minutes and turning to evenly crisp.

Once cooked, remove from the oven and serve as part of a roast. Enjoy.

USEFUL TIP

If you have any surplus potatoes left do not throw them away, use them the following day to make some good old bubble & squeak, just add chopped greens, some seasoning of your choice and gently fry.

Golden Roast Potatoes

Mint Mushrooms in Red Wine Gravy Pie

Who doesn't love a good pie, this combination of mintiness and red wine gravy work perfectly.

EQUIPMENT

- 2 small pie tins (with removable bottoms)
- Medium frying pan
- Basting brush

INGREDIENTS

Makes two small pies

- 375g puff pastry
- 350g field mushrooms
- 1 tbsp dark soy sauce
- 1 tsp garlic granules
- 1 tsp onion granules
- salt & pepper - to taste
- 1 tbsp dried mint
- 1 tbsp olive oil
- 1 tbsp vegan butter
- red wine gravy (see page 182)
- 1 tbsp oat milk

PREPARATION

Chop the field mushrooms into medium sized chunky cubes.

METHOD

Preheat the oven to 220°C/425°F/gas 7

Heat the olive oil in a frying pan over a medium heat, once the oil is hot add the mushrooms and cook for 4 minutes, add the garlic & onion granules and stir in, then add the dark soy sauce and season with the salt & pepper and finally add the dried mint and mix well and cook for another 4 minutes, stirring occasionally. Remove from the heat and leave to sit.

Start heating the red wine gravy over a low heat, stirring occasionally.

Take your two pie tins and grease the insides with the vegan butter. Take the puff pastry, roll it out and cut it into 4 even squares. Insert one of the squares into each of the pie tins (use your fingers to push the pastry into place) fold the excess over the top of the tin. Now cut the two remaining squares so they are the same circumference as the top of the tins (we use a small bowl that's roughly the same size as the pie tin to cut it to shape) and set to the side.

Spoon in the mushrooms and fill 3/4 of the tin, then add the red wine gravy and cover the mushrooms. Now take the two tops you cut out and place on top of each of the pie tins, fold the excess pastry back over the top and pinch to seal the pie. Using a brush, coat the tops of the pie with the oat milk and then pop them in the oven on the middle shelf and cook for 25 minutes or until the pastry has reached a rich golden brown.

Remove from the oven and allow to sit for 2 minutes, then gently remove the pies from the tins.

Serve on it's own as a small lunch or turn it into a main by adding something of your choice.

USEFUL TIP

Serve with either chunky chips or mash.

Mint Mushroom in Red Wine Gravy Pie

Oven Roasted Vegetables

We love this dish as it is one of our go to meals if we are pushed for time and have a busy day. It is simple, quick and simply delicious.

EQUIPMENT

- Large Baking Tray
- Tin Foil

INGREDIENTS

Serves 4-5

- 2 carrots
- 1 red sweet pepper
- 6 baby potatoes
- 1 courgette
- 1/2 fennel
- 2 large tomatoes
- 6 cloves garlic
- 1 parsnip
- 1/4 daikon (white radish)
- 1 white onion
- 1 apple
- 1 tsp smoked paprika
- 2 tsp Italian seasoning
- 1 tsp black pepper
- 1/2 tsp sea salt
- olive oil
- liquid smoke

METHOD

Preheat the oven to 220°C/425°F/gas 7

Roughly chop all the vegetables: carrots, fennel and sweet pepper lengthwise, baby potatoes and tomatoes in halves, parsnip, courgette and daikon into large cubes, peel and slice the apple and onion in quarters.

Place all the vegetables in the baking dish and give them a good mix together.
Sprinkle them with sea salt, black pepper, smoked paprika and Italian seasoning (or your other favourite herbs). Drizzle with olive oil and liquid smoke.

Cover the baking tray with tin foil and place on the middle shelf of the oven and cook for 35 minutes.
After the 35 minutes is up, take the baking tray out and remove the tin foil, stir the vegetables once again and return to the oven for another 15 minutes (without the tin foil).

Remove from the oven and serve.

These scrumptious veggies can be served on their own or as part of a meal.

Oven Roasted Vegetables

Scrumptious Red Wine Gravy

A good gravy can turn the simplest of meals into something special, and this scrumptious red wine gravy delivers just that.

EQUIPMENT

- Medium frying pan
- Medium pot
- Sieve
- Whisk
- Gravy pot

INGREDIENTS

- 1 small leek
- 1 large carrot
- 4 garlic cloves
- 2 celery sticks
- 4 small mushrooms
- 1 tsp rosemary
- 1 tsp thyme
- 1 tsp marjoram
- 400ml red wine
- 1 litre vegetable stock
- 2 tbsp tomato puree
- 1 tsp Marmite
- 1 tbsp miso
- 2 tbsp brown sugar
- 1 tsp English mustard
- 1/2 tsp sea salt
- 1/2 tsp black pepper
- 1 tsp nutritional yeast
- 3 tbsp cornstarch
- 6 tbsp lukewarm water
- splash of olive oil

PREPARATION

Slice the leek.
Peel and chop the carrot.
Peel and mince the garlic.
Slice the celery.
Roughly chop the mushrooms.

Make the vegetable stock (we use Marigold bouillon powder)

METHOD

Pour the olive oil into the pan, add the leek and cook for 2 minutes on medium heat. Add the garlic and cook until the aroma is released. Next, add carrot, celery, mushrooms, marjoram, thyme and rosemary. Stir everything together and cook for around 10 minutes until the vegetables soften. Pour in the red wine and cook until most of the liquid has evaporated.

Pour the vegetable stock into the pan and increase the heat to high, so it starts bubbling. Decrease the heat to low and simmer for 15 minutes stirring occasionally.

Take the pan off the heat and strain the liquid into a bowl, so you are left with a clear stock. Discard the cooked vegetables. Transfer the stock into a medium pot and place back on the hob at medium heat.

Mix in the miso, Marmite, tomato puree, brown sugar, mustard, sea salt and black pepper and bring to a boil.

Meanwhile, mix the cornstarch with lukewarm water and ensure there are no lumps and add to the pot with gravy whisking continuously until all well combined. Let it bubble for 5 minutes, until you have a nice smooth and thick consistency.

Pour the gravy into the jug and serve. Enjoy!

USEFUL TIP

Try this gravy as a mushroom pie filler or serve with chunky chips.

Scrumptious Red Wine Gravy

Sweet Potato Shepards Pie

We absolutely love taking a good old traditional dish and turning it vegan. Here we reinvent the Shepherd's Pie and put our own delicious twist on this classic dish.

EQUIPMENT

- Oven Dish
- Large Pan
- Potato Masher

INGREDIENTS

Serves 4-6

For the Mash
- 740g sweet potatoes
- 2 tbsp vegan butter
- 1 tbsp nutritional yeast
- 1 tsp garlic granules
- 1 tsp onion granules
- 1 tsp cracked black pepper
- pinch of sea salt

For the Base
- olive oil
- 3 garlic cloves
- 1 red onion
- 1 stick of celery
- 1 carrot
- 1 tsp garlic granules
- 1 tsp onion granules
- 1 tsp coriander powder
- 450g of field mushrooms
- half a small glass of red wine
- 2 tsp soy sauce
- 1 tbsp red wine vinegar
- 140g garden peas
- salt to taste
- pepper to taste
- 1x400g tin of lentils

PREPARATION

Peel and chop the sweet potatoes into 2cm cubes.
Peel and chop the garlic cloves.
Peel and dice the red onion.
Finely chop the celery.
Peel and chop the carrot into small cubes.
Chop the field mushrooms into small cubes.
Drain the lentils.

METHOD

Preheat the oven to 220°C/425°F/gas 7.

Place the cubes of sweet potato into a large pan of slightly salted cold water, bring to the boil then simmer for roughly 10 to 15 minutes or until they soften. Drain and leave them to settle for a few minutes, then add the vegan butter, nutritional yeast, garlic granules, onion granules & season with the cracked black pepper & sea salt. Mash until you get a smooth soft texture then set to the side.
Place a pan over a medium heat and

add a good glug of olive oil, add the chopped garlic, red onion, celery & carrot, cook for around 8 minutes or until they have softened. Add the mushrooms to the pan and cook for roughly 6 minutes then add the garlic & onion granules followed by the coriander powder, mix well and cook for another 5 minutes, add the red wine and stir in and allow to cook for 5 minutes to evaporate the alcohol, then add the soy sauce, red wine vinegar, garden peas and season with sea salt and cracked black pepper.

While cooking, drain off the lentils then add them to the pan, mix in well and cook for 3 minutes then remove from the heat.

Take your oven dish and carefully spoon the contents of the pan into it, spreading evenly. Now take the sweet potato mash and spread an even layer across the top (use a fork to create ridges along the top).

Place the oven dish on the middle shelf in the oven and cook for 25 minutes, then remove from the oven and place under the grill for 5 minutes or until you get a nice golden crisp on the top.

Serve with greens of your choice and our red wine gravy goes exceptionally well with this dish (page 182). Enjoy.

Sweet Potato Shepherd's Pie

Veef Wellington

We know how much people love a good old roast dinner so decided to put our very own Veef Wellington together for you to try, we are sure you will enjoy it.

EQUIPMENT

- Baking tray
- Food processor
- Medium frying pan x 2
- Mixing bowl
- Pastry brush

INGREDIENTS

Serves 6-8

- 6 cloves garlic
- 4 portobello mushrooms
- 2 tbsp soy sauce
- 1 tbsp garlic granules
- 1 large red onion
- 300g chestnut mushrooms
- 2 tbsp olive oil
- 2 tbsp white wine vinegar
-   cup red wine
- 180g cooked chestnuts
- 200g walnuts
- 250g cooked puy lentils
- 2 sheets ready-rolled dairy-free shortcrust pastry
- 3 tbsp plant based milk

For the spice mix
- 1 sprig fresh rosemary
- 3-4 sprigs fresh thyme
- 1 tsp marjoram
- 1 tsp sea salt
- 2 tsp black pepper
- 1 tsp sweet paprika
- 2 tsp coconut or brown sugar
- 3 bay leaves

PREPARATION

Peel and mince the garlic.
Peel and finely chop the red onion.
Chop the rosemary and thyme.
Prepare your spice mix by mixing all the ingredients together.
Thinly chop the chestnut mushrooms and set them to the side.
Roughly chop the walnuts.

METHOD

First, prepare Portobello mushrooms. Add a tablespoon of olive oil into a frying pan and heat the oil, place the mushrooms in the pan and fry from both sides for around 2 minutes. Add soy sauce and garlic granules and keep turning until well covered. You can also press them gently with a spatula to remove some of the excess water. Once ready, set aside.

Add a tablespoon of olive oil to the frying pan and place over medium heat. Add the red onion to the pan and saute for around 5 minutes, stirring regularly, until soft.

Next, add chopped chestnut mushrooms to the onion along with your spice mix. Increase the heat and cook until softened and all the liquid has evaporated. Pour the white wine vinegar and red wine into the pan, stir it and cook until most of the liquid has evaporated. Turn off the heat, take out the cooked bay leaves and set it to the side.

Put the cooked chestnuts, lentils and walnuts in the food processor and whizz until the mix resembles sticky breadcrumbs. Mix with the red onion and chestnut mushrooms until you get a dough-like texture.

At this stage, turn the oven on and preheat the oven to 220°C/425°F/gas 7.

Line the baking tray with parchment paper, unroll the shortcrust pastry and place on the baking tray and spread half of the chestnut & mushroom mixture lengthways down the middle of the pastry sheet. Use your hands to mold it into a nice rectangular shape while flattening the top. Leave at least 3-4 cm gap on each side.

Place cooked Portobello mushrooms on top of the stuffing. Top up with the remaining chestnut & mushroom mixture, smooth and shape.

Using a pastry brush, brush a little of the plant-based milk around the pastry edges. Unroll and place the other pastry sheet over the mushroom filling, and gently press to ensure there are no air bubbles. Push the edges down to seal the Wellington, trim any excess pastry making sure you leave around 1cm crust around the base. You can also use a fork to crimp all around the edges to ensure it is sealed properly and make it look nice. Create shapes or patterns from the excess pastry and place them on top of your Wellington to decorate. Brush the Wellington with plant-based milk and make a few air vents in it with a fork.

Put the Wellington in the oven and bake for 30-45 minutes on the middle shelf. Check after 30-35 minutes and if the pastry is a nice brown and looks ready take it out of the oven. If not leave for another 5-10 minutes.

Serve with our Red Wine Gravy (see page 182) and Roast Potatoes (see page 176).

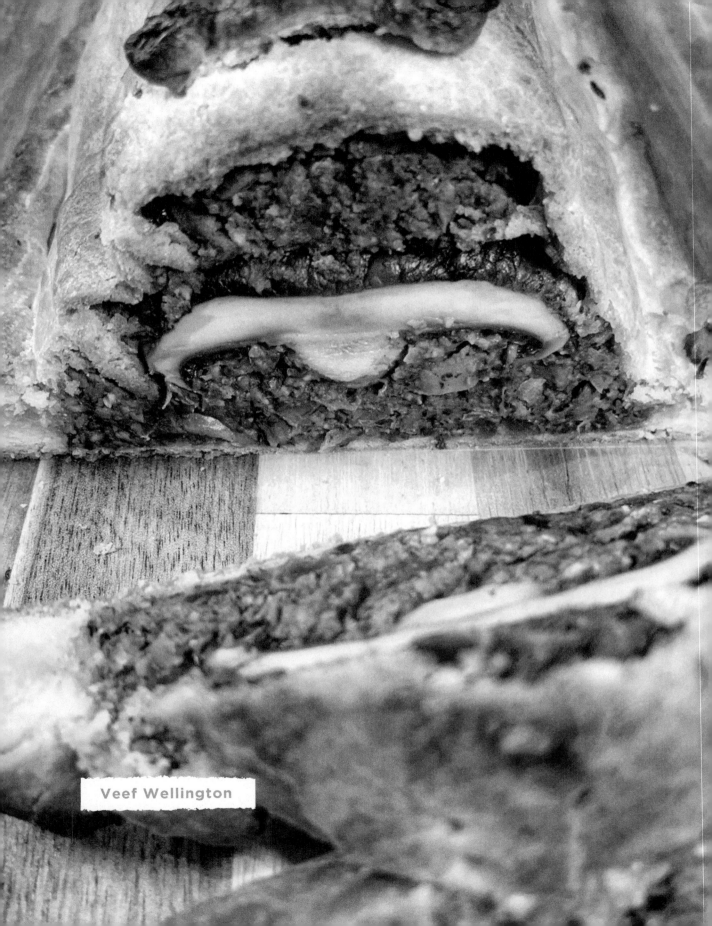

Veef Wellington

Sauces & Dips

Beetroot Hummus

A delicious earthy twist to a traditional hummus with a herby aftertaste of marjoram.

EQUIPMENT

- Blender

INGREDIENTS

Serves 4

- 1 tin chickpea
- 2 small cooked unflavoured beetroots
- 4 garlic cloves
- 2 tbsp tahini
- 1/2 tsp sea salt
- 1/2 tsp cracked black pepper
- 1 tsp smoked paprika
- 1 tsp dried marjoram
- a bit of water

METHOD

Peel and mince the garlic, place all the ingredients into the blender and whizz until you get a smooth texture, adding more water if necessary.

Store in an airtight container for upto 1 week.

Beetroot Hummus

Cashew Sour Cream

A totally awesome alternative to the dairy version, once you try you'll never buy the traditional sour cream again.

EQUIPMENT

- Blender

INGREDIENTS

Makes roughly 150 ml of sour cream

- 1 cup raw cashews
- 1/2 cup water
- 1 lemon
- 1 teaspoon apple cider vinegar
- 1/4 teaspoon sea salt
- 1/4 teaspoon Dijon mustard

PREPARATION

Soak the cashews in warm water for 1 hour.

METHOD

Place all the ingredients into the blender and whizz until you get a fully smooth texture.

Store in an airtight container for up to 1 week.

Cashew Sour Cream

Green Hummus

A very unusual alternative to traditional hummus using green pea instead of chickpea which gives it a much lighter texture and a vibrant colour.

EQUIPMENT

- Blender

INGREDIENTS

Serves 6-8

- 2 cups cooked green pea
- 4 garlic cloves
- 1 small bunch parsley
- 2 tbsp tahini
- 1/2 tsp sea salt
- 1/2 tsp cracked black pepper
- 2 tbsp nutritional yeast
- a bit of water

METHOD

Peel and mince the garlic, roughly chop the parsley and place all the ingredients into the blender and whizz until you get a smooth texture, adding more water if necessary.

Store in an airtight container for upto 1 week.

Green Hummus

Hot Aromatic Green Sauce

We wanted to create a sauce that was bursting with flavour and scrumptious enough that it could be used in a number of different dishes. This simple blend of ingredients did just that.

EQUIPMENT

- Blender

INGREDIENTS

Serves 4

- thumb of fresh ginger
- good handful of fresh coriander
- good handful of fresh mint
- 5 garlic cloves
- pinch of black pepper
- pinch of sea salt
- 1 lime
- 1 tsp chilli flakes
- 1 tbsp of olive oil

PREPARATION

Peel and roughly chop the ginger.
Remove the stems from the coriander and mint.
Peel the garlic cloves.
Juice the lime.

METHOD

Place all of the ingredients into a blender and pulse for roughly 30/40 seconds, add a little water if needed and mix until you reach the desired texture.

Serve & enjoy.

USEFUL TIP

Try getting creative with this delicious sauce and add it to pizzas, tarts, wraps, toast or just as a dipping sauce etc.

Hot Aromatic Green Sauce

Mango Lime & Chilli Ketchup

Lets face it, a bit of ketchup can be a great accompaniment as a side sauce. We absolutely love playing around with our sauces and we came up with this saucy ketchup that has secured a regular spot in our fridge.

EQUIPMENT

- Blender

INGREDIENTS

Makes roughly 500 ml

- 2 mangos
- 2 tbsp maple syrup or coconut sugar
- 1 tsp black pepper
- 1.5 tsp garlic granules
- 1 tsp salt
- 7 vine tomatoes
- 1 lime
- 1 tsp ground nutmeg
- 2 tbsp water
- 1 tsp onion powder
- 2 tsp chilli flakes
- 2 tbsp apple cider vinegar
- 3 heaped tbsp tomato puree

PREPARATION

Skin and dice the mangoes.
Roast the vine tomatoes for 25 minutes.
Juice the lime.

METHOD

Put all of the ingredients into a blender and pulse for roughly 30 seconds,

Check consistency and add more water if necessary until you reach the desired thickness/texture. Best stored in an airtight glass jar, keep refrigerated for upto 1 week.

USEFUL TIP

Once made, if you put the ketchup into a closed glass airtight jar, you can then place it in the oven at 90°C for 1 hour to pasteurise the ketchup, remove from the oven and allow to cool. You can then keep the ketchup refrigerated for up to 6 months.

Mango Lime & Chilli Ketchup

Roasted Red Pepper Hummus

The romano red peppers give this traditional hummus a sweet twist and a rich flavour.

EQUIPMENT

- Blender or Food processor
- Baking tray

INGREDIENTS

Serves 4

- 3 red sweet romano peppers
- 1 tbsp olive oil
- 1 tin chickpea
- 4 garlic cloves
- 2 tbsp tahini
- 1 tsp cumin seeds
- 1/2 tsp sea salt
- 1/2 tsp cracked black pepper
- 1/2 tsp sweet paprika
- 1/2 tsp smoked paprika
- a bit of water

METHOD

Preheat the oven to 220°C/425°F/gas 7

Firstly half the peppers lengthways and deseed them, lay them onto the baking tray and drizzle with the olive oil. Place on the middle shelf and cook for 25 minutes or until the edges start to char. Remove from the oven.

Peel and mince the garlic, place all the ingredients along with the peppers into the blender or food processor and whizz until you get a smooth texture, adding more water if necessary.

Store in an airtight container for upto 1 week.

Roasted Red Pepper Hummus

Saffron Hummus

Saffron is such a beautiful medicinal herb we thought we would bring a bit of life into the standard traditional hummus by adding it.

EQUIPMENT

- Blender or Food Processor
- Pestle & Mortar
- Small Bowl

INGREDIENTS

Serves 4

- 1 tin chickpea
- 4 cloves garlic
- 2 tbsp tahini
- 1 tsp cumin seeds
- 1/2 tsp sea salt
- 1/2 tsp cracked black pepper
- 1/2 tsp sweet paprika
- 1 tsp maple syrup
- pinch of organic saffron
- a bit of water

METHOD

Firstly smash the saffron in a pestle and mortar and then transfer to a small bowl and cover with 1/4 cup of hot water, set aside for 10 minutes.

Peel and mince the garlic, place all the ingredients including the saffron and water from soaking into the blender and whizz until you get a smooth texture, adding more water if necessary.

Store in an airtight container for upto 1 week.

Saffron Hummus

Desserts

Apple Cinnamon & Walnut Slice

This was just simply one of those moments when an idea pops into your head whilst eating another dish containing some of the ingredients. And we absolutely loved it.

EQUIPMENT

- Baking Tray
- Parchment Paper
- Saucepan
- Mixing Bowl
- Grater

INGREDIENTS

Makes 4 slices

- 1 Roll of Puff Pastry
- 1/4 cup (2oz/57g) butter
- 4 apples peeled
- 2/3 cup (4oz/115g) coconut sugar
- 2 teaspoons of cinnamon
- Pinch of salt
- Zest of 1 Lemon
- 3/4 cup of Walnut halves
- 1 tbsp Oat Milk
- cinnamon sugar for dusting (optional)

PREPARATION

Peel, core & grate the apples.
Grate the lemon and put the zest to the side.
Chop the walnut halves.

METHOD

Preheat the oven to 200°C/400°F/ gas 6

Line the baking tray with parchment paper.

Using a shallow saucepan over a medium heat, add the butter, grated apples, coconut sugar, cinnamon, pinch of salt & lemon zest. Cook for 2-3 minutes or until most of the liquids have reduced and the grated apple softens, transfer to a bowl then set to the side to cool down. Add the walnut halves to the bowl with the cooked apples and mix well. Once cooled you can keep this in the fridge for upto 5 days if you want to.

Take the Puff Pastry and roll it out, cut the sheet into 4 even rectangles and gently separate them. For each of the rectangle sheets, carefully spoon the apple mix into the centre.

Brush one half of the pastry edges with the oat milk, fold the pastry over and press and seal using the edge of a fork. Carefully slice the pastry across the top a few times for venting.

Gently place the slices onto the baking tray and then brush the oat milk across the top and finish with a generous sprinkle of cinnamon sugar. Cook for 20-25 minutes or until they turn puffy and golden.

Serve on its own or with a generous spoon of vegan vanilla ice cream or a delicious yoghurt of your choice.

Enjoy.

USEFUL TIP

If you have any of the filling left, get creative and try using as a pizza topping, add in wraps, sandwiches etc

Apple, Cinnamon & Walnut Slice

Chocolate Flapjacks

These flapjacks simply are a nutritious powerhouse. Oats provide the required fibre and nourish the nervous system, maple syrup is full of essential minerals, blackstrap molasses are an abundant source of iron, almond butter is rich in omega 3 and 6 fatty acids, and finally banana provides that additional natural sweetness and lots of potassium.

And you can have it any time of the day, not only as a healthier dessert option!

EQUIPMENT

- Mixing bowl
- Spatula
- Whisk
- 20 cm square baking tray
- Airtight container

INGREDIENTS

Makes 12-16

- 1/2 cup almond butter (or any other nut or seed butter)
- 1/2 cup maple syrup
- 1/4 cup blackstrap molasses
- 1 large ripe banana
- 1/2 tsp baking powder
- 1/4 tsp sea salt
- 2 1/2 heaped cups rolled oats
- 50g vegan dark chocolate

PREPARATION

Line a 20 cm / 8" square baking tin (or similar) with baking paper. Mash the banana until you get a smooth texture.

METHOD

Preheat the oven to 170°C/325°F/gas 3

Whisk the peanut butter, maple syrup and molasses in a mixing bowl until the mixture is smooth. Mix in the mashed banana, baking soda and salt.

Finally, add in the oats. Stir until all the oats are evenly coated in the mixture and the 'dough' is sticky but not overly wet (if it's too wet, add a little bit more oats).

Transfer the mixture to the baking tray. Press the mixture really well to make sure the flapjack holds together after baking.
Bake for about 30 minutes, until the oats start turning golden brown around the edges. Remove from the

oven and press the flapjack again while warm using a spatula.

Melt the chocolate over a water bath (place the chocolate into a heatproof bowl and put the bowl into a pot of water, bring the water to a boil then turn the heat off and let the boiled water melt the chocolate). Drizzle over the cooled flapjack and let it set. Cut into bars and store in the airtight container for up to a week.

USEFUL TIP

Try adding chopped dry fruits, like apricots, dates, cranberries or chocolate chunks before baking, mix well and be ready for a completely new experience.

Chocolate Flapjacks

Gluten-Free Beetroot Brownies

Beetroot and chocolate? Yes, it's a match made in heaven. Roasted beetroot brings well needed moisture into this simple brownie recipe with almond flour as a base, without changing its chocolate rich taste.

USEFUL TIP

Safe for those with gluten allergy/intolerance, as well as nut allergies, if you use ground sunflower and any seed butter instead of almond ingredients in the recipe.

EQUIPMENT

- Small pot
- Blender
- Knife
- Square or rectangular baking tin

INGREDIENTS

Makes roughly 12 brownies

- 2 small beetroots
- 2 cups pitted dates
- 1/2 plant-based milk
- 1/2 cups almond butter
- 3 cups ground almonds (or sunflower seeds)
- 3/4 cup raw cacao
- 1 tsp sea salt
- 2 tsp baking powder
- 1 block of vegan chocolate

PREPARATION

Put the beetroots into a small pot, cover with water and boil for around 30 minutes or until soft. Soak the dates in freshly boiled water for 15 minutes.
Line a square or rectangular baking tin with greased baking paper.

METHOD

Preheat the oven to 180°C/350°F/gas 4

Mix the dry ingredients in the large bowl first (ground almonds, raw cacao, sea salt and baking powder).

Chop the chocolate bar into small chunks and mix half of it with dry ingredients.

Drain the dates. Put them into the blender along with the almond butter, plant-based milk and beetroots and blend until smooth. Mix with the dry ingredients until well combined and smooth and transfer to a baking tin. Sprinkle it with the remaining chopped chocolate.

Bake for 20 minutes on the middle shelf of the oven. They should be slightly cracked at the top and slightly firm inside but still quite gooey – be careful not to overcook!

Once cooked, remove from the oven and cut into squares. Serve with vanilla ice cream and fresh raspberries. Store in the fridge for up to 5 days.

Gluten Free Beetroot Brownies

Raw Vegan Chocolate Avocado Cake

It's a perfect treat for all chocolate lovers out there, with no refined sugar, nuts, or gluten, enriched with adaptogenic herbs like maca, Siberian ginseng and burdock root to give you more energy and help with stress. Exquisitely rich, smooth and creamy chocolate cake with no taste of avocado that will leave you wanting more.

EQUIPMENT

- Food processor
- Blender
- 22cm cake tin
- Kitchen scales
- Spatula
- Small pot

INGREDIENTS

Serves 12-16

For the base
- 180g dates
- 150g coconut flakes
- 50g sunflower seeds

For the chocolate filling
- 180 cup dates
- 2 hass avocados
- 120g raw cacao powder
- 170g coconut sugar
- 110g coconut oil, melted
- 3 tbsp maple syrup
- 1 tsp vanilla extract
- 200g coconut cream (i.e. Biona Organic)
- 30g lucuma powder
- 10g Siberian ginseng powder
- 10g burdock root powder
- 10g maca powder

PREPARATION

Soak 1 cup of dates for the chocolate filling in warm water for 1 hour.

Soak the coconut cream pouch in boiling water for 30 minutes or until the cream is completely soft.

METHOD

Blend the base ingredients in the food processor until you get a dough texture. Spread across the bottom of the cake tin and put it in the fridge while you make the chocolate filling.

The exact quantities are important in this filling to achieve the perfect and fully set texture. Measure 110g of coconut oil and melt in the small pot, and pour into the blender. Strain the dates and add to the oil. Cut the coconut cream pouch and squeeze out its content into the blender (IMPORTANT: it must be coconut cream, not coconut milk in the tin). Add all the remaining ingredients and blend until completely smooth.

Take the base out of the fridge and top with chocolate filling. Use the spatula to scrape the blender walls and smooth out the top.

Place back in the fridge for 3-4 hours to set.

Serve with grated dark chocolate and ice cream. Enjoy!

USEFUL TIP

It's a large cake so feel free to portion it and freeze it. It keeps well for up to 6 months. Allow 1 hour to defrost.
You can omit the herbs or simply use one or two or even replace with your favourite vegan protein powder instead.

Raw Vegan Chocolate Avocado Cake

Raw Vegan Salted Caramel Apple Tart

Apples, cinnamon and caramel are simply divine and this raw vegan tart tastes just that. A beautiful light combination that will satisfy your sweet tooth immediately.

EQUIPMENT

- Food processor
- Blender
- 20cm tart tin
- Mixing bowl

INGREDIENTS

Serves 8-10

- 4-5 sweet apples

For the base
- 1 cup walnuts
- 1 cup dates

Salted caramel sauce
- 3/4 cup dates
- 1/4 cup peanut butter
- 1 tsp miso
- 1 tbsp maple syrup
- 1/2 tsp cinnamon
- 1/4 - 1/2 cup water

PREPARATION

Place the walnuts and dates into the food processor and process until you get a smooth but still crumbly texture.

Transfer into a tart tin and spread evenly at the bottom and around the edges. Put into the freezer for 15 minutes to set.

METHOD

Peel and grate the apples and place them in the mixing bowl.

Place all the salted caramel sauce ingredients with 1/4 cup of water to start with into the blender and whizz until smooth, adding more water if necessary.

Take out 3 tablespoons and set aside in a small bowl. Mix the rest of the sauce with the grated apple.

Take the tart base out of the freezer and top with the salted caramel apple filling. Drizzle with the saved sauce and put into the fridge for 3 hours to set.

Serve with your favourite vegan vanilla ice cream. Enjoy!

USEFUL TIP

If you have a nut allergy, use 1 1/2 cup of sunflower seeds in the base and hemp seed butter instead of peanut butter in the salted caramel sauce.

Raw Vegan Salted Caramel Apple Tart

Seeded Energy Balls infused with Orange & Cardamom

These little beauties are a must have in our fridge, perfect for when you are on the go and in need of an energy boost. Delightfully tasty & very nutritious.

EQUIPMENT

- Blender or food processor
- Small pan

INGREDIENTS

Makes roughly 20 -25

- 1/2 cup dates
- 1/2 cup dried apricots
- 1/2 cup pumpkin seeds, lightly toasted in a dry pan
- 1/2 cup sunflower seeds
- 1/2 cup white sesame seeds
- 1 tsp ground cardamom
- 1 pinch mineral salt
- 1 tsp fresh organic orange zest
- 2-3 tbsp melted coconut oil
- 1/3 cup whole white sesame seeds, ground flax seeds, or unsweetened, shredded dried coconut to coat the finished balls (optional)
- Optional taste options: carob, cacao, matcha powder, spirulina

PREPARATION

Lightly toast the pumpkin seeds in a small pan without oil, once toasted transfer to a bowl and allow to cool. Soak the dried apricots in hot water for roughly 15-20 minutes.

METHOD

Add the pumpkin seeds, sunflower and sesame seeds to a blender or food processor. Add the cardamom and salt to the seeds and combine well. If you are adding carob, cacao, and/or spirulina powder, do so now and mix well.

Drain the dried apricots and add them along with the dates, coconut oil and orange zest to the blender or food processor and blend until you get a dough-like texture.

Using a teaspoon, scoop up a spoonful of the mixture and roll into a walnut-sized ball in the palms of your hands. If the balls don't easily stick together, add a bit more oil. If too wet, grind more sesame or sunflower seeds to thicken the mixture.

For a nutritive, decorative touch, roll the balls in either whole sesame seeds, ground flax seeds, and/ or shredded coconut. This also prevents the balls from being sticky on the outside.

USEFUL TIP

If you don't have time to roll the balls, opt to make bars by pressing the mixture into a lightly oiled, glass 9 x 9" baking dish.Cut and enjoy as needed.

Seeded Energy Balls Infused with Orange & Cardamom

Upside Down Apple Cake

We love using seasonal fruit and vegetables in recipes. When it comes round to autumn, apples are one of our favourites. Although these days it is easy to forget that fruit is seasonal because you can buy it all year round, our Fast Apple Cake is perfect for those cold autumn evenings. Sweet with a hint of spice, this quick and easy cake is ready to eat in just over an hour.

EQUIPMENT

- 20cm Cake Tin
- Mixing Bowl
- Mixing Jug

INGREDIENTS

Dry

- 180g (1.5 cups) spelt flour (if you prefer a gluten-free version, you can use gluten-free flour + 3/4tsp xanthan gum)
- 134g (3/4 cups) coconut sugar
- 3/4 tsp baking powder
- 1 tsp cinnamon
- a pinch of salt

Wet

- 125ml olive oil
- 50ml warm water
- 1 tablespoon of apple cider vinegar

- 3 apples

METHOD

Preheat the oven to 190°C/375°F/gas 5

Prepare the apples first. Peel them, cut into quarters and remove the seeds,then cut them into slices.
Mix the dry ingredients in a bowl. Add the wet ingredients into a jug and thoroughly mix . Then slowly add to the dry ingredients and mix well until you get a smooth consistency. The batter will be very thick but don't worry, Once you add the apples these will release their moisture as they bake.

Line the base of a 9 in (23cm) non-stick cake tin with greaseproof paper. Arrange some of the apples in a circular pattern to cover the bottom of the cake tin.

Spoon the batter into the tin and spread evenly. Be careful not to disrupt the apple pattern on the bottom, Now gently fold the remaining apples into the batter. Place on the middle shelf of the oven and bake for 40-45mins.

When ready, the cake should be

slightly browned on top and slightly shrunken away from the edges of the cake tin.

Leave in the tin to cool down for about 5 minutes and then turn it out onto a rack so that the apple pattern is now on top.

Once it has cooled, gently peel off the greaseproof paper to reveal the apple pattern.

Dust with cinnamon or powdered coconut sugar. Serve with a scoop of vanilla ice cream and enjoy.

Upside Down Apple Cake

Very Berry Cheesecake

Baked vegan cheesecake with a creamy filling and juicy berries. It really has the creaminess of a regular cheesecake and is simply delicious!

EQUIPMENT

- Mixing bowl
- Spatula
- 20cm cake tin
- Small pot

INGREDIENTS

Serves 10-12

For the crust
- 1 1/2 cups plain flour or gluten-free flour
- 1/2 cup almond flour, or substitute with more flour
- 1/4 cup coconut sugar
- 3/4 cup vegan butter

For the cheesecake filling
- 2 cups cashews
- 250g silken tofu
- 1/2 cup agave syrup
- 1/2 cup dairy free yoghurt, such as coconut, soy or almond
- 1/4 cup plant-based milk
- 1 tablespoon cornstarch/flour
- 1/2 lemon
- 2 teaspoons vanilla extract
- pinch of sea salt

For the berries jelly
- 1 1/2 cups frozen wild berries
- 3 tablespoons agave syrup (optional)
- 1 tablespoon cornstarch/flour

PREPARATION

Line the bottom and sides of a spring-form or loose-bottom cake tin.
Soak the cashews for 1 hour.
Juice 1/2 lemon.

METHOD

Preheat the oven to 180°C/350°F/gas 4

To make the crust, mix all the crust ingredients until well combined and has a smooth sticky consistency. Firmly press the mixture into the bottom and sides of the lined cake tin so it's about 1cm thick. Place the crust in the preheated oven on the middle shelf and bake for 10-15 minutes or until slightly golden and it's dry to the touch. Keep checking it as the edges burn easily. Once done, set aside.

While the crust is baking, prepare

the cheesecake filling, by adding all the ingredients to a blender and blend until it's completely smooth. Check with a spatula that there are no lumps and blend for a bit longer if needed. Pour the cheesecake filling into the baked crust. Gently tap the cheesecake firmly on the kitchen counter a few times to remove any air bubbles.

Bake the cheesecake on the middle shelf for 45-50 minutes. If the crust is browning too quickly, cover the cheesecake with a baking tray. The cheesecake is ready when the filling is no longer liquid, however it should still wiggle a bit in the middle. Let the cheesecake cool in the oven with the door slightly opened for 1-2 hours (this is to prevent the cake cooling too quickly which would make the middle of the cake collapse). Once the time has passed, take the cheesecake out of the oven and allow it to cool down completely. Once it reaches room temperature, you can place it in the fridge and allow it to fully set.

Add the berries and agave syrup to a small saucepan and place it over medium heat, mixing occasionally until the berries are fully defrosted. In a cup, mix 1 tablespoon of cornstarch with 1 1/2 tablespoon of water until

there are no lumps. Next, add it to the berries, decrease the heat to low and stir until smooth and thickened. Remove from the heat and allow it to cool.

Take the cheesecake out of the fridge and remove the cake tin, place the cheesecake on a plate then spread the berry jelly evenly across the top. Return the cheesecake to the fridge for a further 30 minutes to allow the berry jelly to set.

Serve and enjoy!

USEFUL TIP

The cheesecake can be kept in an airtight container in the fridge for up to 4 days. Try different toppings instead of berries, because it is delicious with mangoes, peaches, and even pears.

Very Berry Cheesecake

Drinks

lavender lemonade

This is a delightfully refreshing refined sugar free drink with a strong hint of lavender that can be enjoyed all year round.

EQUIPMENT

- 2 Large Bowls
- Strainer

INGREDIENTS

- 5 tbsp lavender
- 3 tbsp maple syrup
- 2 large lemons
- 1 cup of boiling water
- 1.5 litre cold water
- ice cubes

USEFUL TIP

If you like your lemonade to have a bit of fizz you can replace the cold water with sparkling water.

METHOD

Place the lavender, maple syrup and boiling water in a bowl, give it a stir and let it infuse for at least half an hour. The longer you allow it to infuse the better.

Strain the mixture into the second bowl and add the lemon juice, cold water and ice cubes, give a good stir then pour into a jug. Enjoy!

Lavender Lemonade

Smoothies

Smoothies are a perfect way to incorporate a good portion of fresh vegetables, fruits, healthy fats, protein, fibre and herbs into our daily diet. They are quick to make, filling and can easily replace breakfast or lunch, while on the go, or simply be a nutritious addition to them.

EQUIPMENT

- Blender
- Electric or hand juicer

METHOD

Brew 1 tablespoon of organic nettle tea in 1 cup of boiling water for 10 minutes and then cool down.
Juice lemons and set aside
Roughly chop the greens, pear and banana and place in the blender with the nettle infusion, Omega 3,6,9 or flaxseed oil, lemon juice, and pumpkin and milk thistle seeds.
Blend until smooth. Drink right away or pour into an airtight jug or bottle and store in the fridge for up to 24h.

Cells Regeneration Greenery

INGREDIENTS

- 1 handful of spinach
- 1 handful of rocket
- 1 handful mint
- 1 handful parsley
- 1 pear
- 1 tbsp Omega 3,6,9 oil blend (or flaxseed oil)
- 1 tbsp pumpkin seeds
- 1 tbsp milk thistle seeds
- 2 lemons
- 1/2 banana
- 1 cup of nettle infusion

Anti-inflammatory Berry Blend

INGREDIENTS

- 1/2 pineapple
- 1 cup of frozen wild berries
- 1 tbsp omega 3,6,9 oil blend
- 2 limes
- 4 medjool dates
- 1 tbsp cranberry powder
- 1 cup rosehip infusion

METHOD

Brew 1 tablespoon of organic rosehip tea in 1 cup of boiling water for 10 minutes and then cool down.

Juice limes and set aside.

Peel and roughly chop the pineapple. Place all ingredients in the blender and blend until smooth. Drink right away or pour into an airtight jug or bottle and store in the fridge for up to 24h.

Dance in the Sun

INGREDIENTS

- 1/2 pineapple
- 1 mango
- 1/2 banana
- 1 cup plant based milk
- 1 tsp turmeric
- 1 tbsp omega 3,6,9 oil blend
- 1 tbsp siberian ginseng
- 1 tbsp oats

METHOD

Peel and roughly cut pineapple and mango.
Slice the banana.
Place all ingredients in the blender and blend until smooth. It's quite a thick smoothie, so add more plant based milk, if you prefer a more liquid texture. It keeps well in the fridge for up to 24h.

Smoothies

Tamarind Lemonade

A refreshing and zingy lemonade with a deep tamarind taste and a hint of lemon and lime to enjoy any time of the year.

EQUIPMENT

- 2 Litre jug or pitcher

INGREDIENTS

Makes around 2 Litres

- 2 heaped tablespoons tamarind paste
- 2 lemons
- 2 limes
- 3 – 5 tablespoons maple syrup adjust to taste
- 1.5 – 2 litres water
- 1/2 tsp vanilla extract
- Mint leaves

METHOD

Squeeze the juice from one lemon and one lime in a jug/pitcher or large serving bowl. Next, add the tamarind paste and mix well. Add the water and stir well to combine.

You can also strain this mixture if you do not want the pulp and fibre in the juice.

Add vanilla extract and maple syrup starting from 3 tablespoons and adjusting to taste.

Slice the other lemon and lime and add to the jug/pitcher along with the mint leaves. Chill to let it infuse for a couple of hours. Serve with ice in tall glasses, garnished with lemon/lime slices.

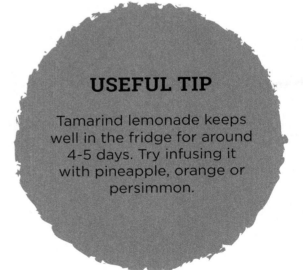

USEFUL TIP

Tamarind lemonade keeps well in the fridge for around 4-5 days. Try infusing it with pineapple, orange or persimmon.

Tamarind Lemonade

Winter Fruit Compote

A traditional Eastern European hot non-alcoholic warming fruit punch that is always served during Christmas, but it's so delicious, that it would be rude not to have it all the time during cold winter months.

USEFUL TIP

Tamarind lemonade keeps well in the fridge for around 4-5 days. Try infusing it with pineapple, orange or persimmon.

EQUIPMENT

- Deep Pot
- Strainer
- Large Bowl

INGREDIENTS

- 2l water
- 2 apples
- 2 pears
- 100g dried apricots
- 80g of prunes
- 50g medjool dates
- 50g cranberries
- 7 cloves
- 1 cinnamon stick
- 1/2 lemon
- 1 orange

METHOD

Put the apples, pears and dried fruits in the pot and cover with 2l water, Add the cloves and cinnamon sticks.

Place the pot over medium heat and bring to the boil and then decrease the heat to low and simmer for 30-45 minutes.

Part of the liquid will evaporate and you should be left with around 1300-1500ml of compote.

Strain the compote into a large bowl and add the lemon and orange juice, give a good stir then transfer to an airtight jug or bottle. It will be a strong compote that you can mix with hot or cold water in proportions 1:1 (or according to your taste).

PREPARATION

Cut apples and pears into quarters. Juice half a lemon and 1 orange and set aside.

Winter Fruit Compote

Final Words

First and foremost we would like to thank you for purchasing our book. We hope the content that we are sharing with you in this book takes you on an exciting journey which is both educational and one that also encourages you to cook outside of the box. You will discover just how easy it is to enjoy absolutely scrumptious meals in the comfort of your own home.

We would absolutely love for you to share any of our meals that you recreate and tag us on Instagram: https://www.instagram.com/greenlicious.cooking

Printed in Great Britain
by Amazon

76320589R00133